A Place
Called
Doña Ana

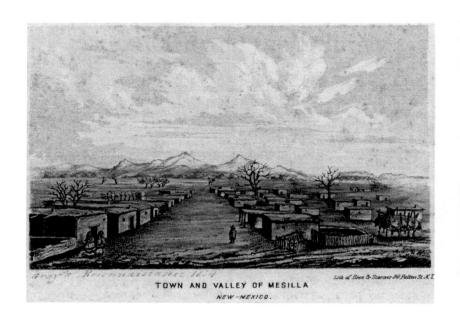

TOWN AND VALLEY OF MESILLA
NEW-MEXICO.

Village of Doña Ana
Sketched during American Surveyor Andrew B. Gray's
reconnaissance for the Boundary Commission in 1854. (See
Chapter 6 for more details.) Courtesy of New Mexico State
University Library, Archives and Special Collections, Image
No. 03390024.

A Place
Called
Doña Ana

by

James J. (Pete) Drexler

13-digit ISBN: *9781708925659*

Table of Contents

List of Illustrations

Photos:

Maps.

Preface

This book follows the development of the Village of Doña Ana, the Mesilla Valley and the surrounding region from its first settlement through the founding of permanent towns. Some settlements earlier than Doña Ana are discussed but those were abandoned due to Apache attacks.

The Village of Doña Ana was the first "European" settlement in the southern part of the present state of New Mexico and was authorized by the governor of Chihuahua in 1839 when the area was still a part of Mexico. However, the village was not officially settled until 1842 or 1843. The County of Doña Ana came into being in 1852 after the United States acquired the area from Mexico as a result of the Mexican War in 1848 and was organized into the Territory of New Mexico in 1850 as part of the Compromise of 1850. In 1855 the county was expanded to include the area of the Gadsden Purchase. At that time, the Territory of New Mexico extended from the present eastern state line of New Mexico to the eastern state line of the present state of California at the Colorado River. Doña Ana County encompassed the entire southern part of the Territory with the Texas state line at Latitude 32° forming the southern boundary to the Rio Grande, and the Mexico international border forming the southern boundary from the Rio Grande to the Colorado River. The northern boundary of Doña Ana County was formed by Latitude 33° (approximately) from the eastern New Mexico Territory line westward to the Gila River just below Fort Thomas (now Arizona). From there, the northern boundary followed the Gila River to its confluence with the Colorado River at Yuma.

Acknowledgements

I want to thank my sister, Joan Richey, and my daughter, Dr. Kristin Anne Drexler, for reviewing this book in its unfinished form and for proofreading the finished version. Their contributions are appreciated. I would also like to express my gratitude to Daniel Aranda and Eric Fuller who opened their archives for me when I was first beginning this task. Perhaps the person who deserves the most gratitude is Senator Mary Jane Garcia who has inspired me - and many others - with her tireless work promoting the Doña Ana Historical Preservation Committee.

Books by the author:

Coronado's Journey to the Seven Cities of Gold. 2015
ISBN: 9780977983117

The Route and Ordeal of Cabeza de Vaca. 2016
ISBN: 9781539895701

Coronado's Route to Cíbola. 2017
ISBN: 9781974052639

Horses to Rockets. 2018
ISBN: 9781726367608

A Place Called Doña Ana. 2019
ISBN: 9781708925659 (Color)
ISBN: 9781673284287 (B&W)

Chapter 1

A Short Early History

The land that was to become Doña Ana County encompassed the entire southern portions of the present States of New Mexico and Arizona. This region was inhabited by mankind for an untold number of millennia[1], but the first Europeans to visit were Cabeza de Vaca party[2] in 1536, Marcos de Niza and Estevan de Dorantes in 1539 and the entire Coronado Expedition[3] in 1540.

The site which became the first permanent, official town within the confines of the present Doña Ana County, New Mexico is the village of Doña Ana, about six miles north of Las Cruces. The first Spaniards[4] to visit this site, sometime in 1581, were probably the group[5] composed of Friars Augustín Rodríguez, Francisco Lopez, and Juan de Santa María along with their military escort, Capt. Franscisco Sánchez Chamuscado and perhaps 12 soldiers (names are known[6] for eight of them: Pedro Bustamante, Hernan Gallegos, Felipe Escalante, Hernando Barrundo, Pedro Sanchez de Chavez, Juan Sanchez, a Herrera and a Fuensalida), eight to fifteen Indian servants and a mestizo, Juan Bautista. This was a group of Franciscan *padres* that had left San Bartolomé on June 6, 1581 and had come up the Rio Grande from the confluence of the Rio Conchos (probably following the same path as Cabeza de Vaca on the east side of Rio Grande).

While Cabeza de Vaca crossed the Rio Grande near the present site of El Paso on his westward trek, the group of *padres* continued its journey northward, still going up the east side of the river, probably. Chamuscado and his soldiers returned to

---

1   MacNeish and Libby. Pendejo Cave, 2003, p 3.
2   J.J. Drexler. The Route and Ordeal of Cabeza de Vaca.
3   J.J. Drexler. The Coronado Expedition to the Seven Cities of Gold.
4   P.M. Baldwin. A Short History of the Mesilla Valley, p 314.
5   L.B. Prince. Historical Sketches of New Mexico, p 150. .
6   H.H. Bancroft. The Works of Hubert Howe Bancroft, Vol 17, p 75

Mexico after the group reached a pueblo just south of the present site of Bernalillo (at, or very near, the place where Coronado had spent the winters of 1541 and 1542). Chamuscado most likely followed the same route on the southbound journey as they took on the northbound journey. The three *padres* were killed soon after Chamuscado left them in the north country.

When Chamuscado again reached the valley of San Bartolomé, the people there immediately began to make plans for relief of the Franciscan *padres*, but it was not until December 10, 1582 (or November 10, 1582 according to Bancroft[7]) that Don Antonio de Espejo[8] left with a much larger expedition, apparently following the same path as the previous expedition. Probably sometime in January 1583, the Espejo expedition became the second group of Spaniards to pass through the site of the present Doña Ana. Espejo returned to Mexico from the pueblos in the north by way of the Rio Pecos, so did not pass Doña Ana again.

The third group (and by far the largest) to pass through the Doña Ana region was the Don Juan de Oñate expedition on its way to colonize the northern part of New Mexico in 1598. This expedition started at Santa Bárbara in the San Bartolomé valley and included[9] 400 men with 130 families, perhaps 10 priests, "many" Negros slaves and Indians, 83 wagons and 7,000 cattle. They left the vicinity of Santa Bárbara about the middle of January 1598 and instead of following the southern bank of Rio Conchos to its confluence with the Rio Grande, as the two previous expeditions had done, Oñate's expedition crossed the Rio Conchos just east of the present city of Chihuahua on Feb. 7, 1598. They then proceeded northward on the trail that would later become known as the "Camino Real" and reached the west (right) side of the Rio Grande on April 20, 1598.

There is some question as to exactly where the expedition first approached the Rio Grande. Hal Jackson[10] has

---

7   H.H. Bancroft. The Works of Hubert Howe Bancroft, Vol 17, p 81
8   L.B. Prince. Historical Sketches of New Mexico, p 153.
9   H.H. Bancroft. The Works of Hubert Howe Bancroft, Vol 17, p 12
10   H. Jackson.. Following the Royal Road, 2006. p 101

traced Oñate's route and reports that this point was at Guadalupe Bravos, Mexico about 8.5 miles south of Fabens, Texas or about 40 miles southeast of El Paso, Texas. Bancroft's opinion[11] is that the expedition crossed the Rio Grande near the present site of El Paso, which agrees with Jackson's routing. However, the more commonly held belief is that the Camino Real continued almost due north from Chihuahua to Juarez so that the first place the expedition would have met the Rio Grande would have been at the El Paso location. [But that particular routing of the El Camino Real did not occur until sometime later when the road through the sand dunes was developed.] In that case, they would have continued traveling on the west side of the Rio Grande and may have crossed that river at Vado, New Mexico. There is a third possible routing of Oñate's expedition: he could have stayed on the west side of the river through the present site of Mesilla and could have gone up to the present site of Picacho village before crossing the river near Doña Ana. The only "evidence" for this latter routing is the local "common knowledge" of "Oñate's Trail" and the fact that an old Indian trade route crossed the river near Picacho. My own opinion is that Jackson and Bancroft were correct in Oñate's routing.

After his first encounter with the Rio Grande, Oñate formally took possession of all the surrounding region on April 30, 1598 while still on western (the "right") side of the Rio Grande. He then traveled 8.5 leagues (about 23 miles) up river before crossing the river. This implies that the spot where he took possession was probably somewhere between San Elizario and Socorro (both are now in Texas on the east side of the Rio Grande, but since Oñate's time the changing course of the Rio Grande had both sites on the west side of the river). On May 4 he forded the river at "Vado de los Puertos[12]" which can be translated as "ford of the mountain pass" and which is a good description of the crossing at the El Paso location and a somewhat reasonable description of the crossing at Picacho but which would not describe the Vado crossing, at all.

11   H.H. Bancroft. The Works of Hubert Howe Bancroft, Vol 17, p 127
12   H.H. Bancroft. The Works of Hubert Howe Bancroft, Vol 17, p 126

Continuing the journey north, up the Rio Grande following an old Indian trade route, Oñate got as far as San Juan Pueblo just below the mouth of the Rio Grande Gorge where he established the settlement of San Gabriel which was the first capital of New Mexico. Several other settlements followed in the next 80 years and included Santa Fe, Taos, Pecos, Socorro and a host of other, smaller communities. In 1680 the Pueblo Indians revolted, killing many of the Spanish and chasing the remainder southward to the El Paso del Norte region, which had developed into a major city along the El Camino Real. On the retreat southward, the remaining settlers under Governor Antonio de Otermín camped at the paraje at Doña Ana[13] on February 4, 1682.

When Diego de Vargas reconquered northern New Mexico in 1693, he did so with the help of more that 800 civilian men, women and children most of whom presumably had been among those who had accompanied Gov. Otermín southward to the El Paso region after the 1680 Indian Revolt. Another 26 families recruited from the Parral area followed in 1694. The first of these groups brought[14] 12 wagons and drove 900 head of cattle but it is not recorded how many wagons or cattle accompanied the second group. All of de Vargas' settlers would have passed through the Mesilla Valley and the *paraje* (see sidebar below) at Doña Ana on their way north and represents the last large group to have done so.

These Spanish people's descendants have maintained a continuous presence in northern New Mexico since de Vargas' resettlement. On the other hand, the southern part of New Mexico (which included the part of the present state of Chihuahua down to El Carrizal) has been occupied since Oñate came to the area in 1598 (or soon thereafter).

The next major influx of people into the Doña Ana region occurred in 1842 when the Doña Ana Bend Colony Grant was issued to 166 settlers from El Paso del Norte. That was followed closely by USA military men in 1846 when the USA declared

13   J.J. Bowden. Spanish and Mexican Land Grants, 1971. p 75
14   M.L. Moorhead. New Mexico's Royal Road, 1958. p 40

Paraje

A *paraje* is a campsite that provided relief for both people and animals along the trail for overnight rests. These campsites would have provided a source of water, firewood, forage and perhaps game to supplement the traveler's diet. Some *parajes*, such as the one at Doña Ana, were well established and used by many of the caravans traveling the Camino.

war on Mexico (see Chapter 3) over the issue of Texas' claim of land that included the village of Doña Ana. Anglos invaded New Mexico at that time and soon had a military post at the village of Doña Ana. When the war ended in 1848, many of the military men stayed in the area and some brought their families or married local girls and their descendants (as well as many other Anglos) have been in the Doña Ana region ever since. New Mexico became a Territory of the US in 1850 and became a State in 1912.

Doña Ana

Chapter 2

El Camino Real
de Tierra Adentro
in Doña Ana County

As soon as Oñate established his colony in the Española valley of northern New Mexico and established its first capital at San Gabriel just north of the San Juan Pueblo (now called Ohkay Owingeh), supplies necessary for its support started flowing from Mexico. The route taken by those supply caravans followed basically the route taken by the Oñate expedition. A major difference in the routing of El Camino Real occurred when the cities of Chihuahua and El Paso del Norte (now Juarez) came into existence and road through the sand dunes between the two cities was developed. El Camino Real started using that routing to El Paso del Norte and it continued to be used for the next 300 years until the coming of the railroads in the 1880s. However, the trail through El Paso Canyon just north of the Vado de los Puertos proved to be very difficult and the caravans soon started using a route that stayed west of the Rio Grande and west of the Mule Drivers Mountain (now called Mt. Cristo Rey) and crossed the Rio Grande at the "upper" crossing, about 6 miles northwest of El Paso del Norte (Juarez). In later years[1] a road that stayed west of the river was developed and could have been a major branch of El Camino Real after it was opened. It appears that the trail to the east of the river continued to be the main route of El Camino Real de Tierra Adentro until the caravans of *carretas* and wagons stopped running between Chihuahua and Santa Fe. But that routing, too, had many branches made necessary by flooding of the river or the washing out of paths and perhaps due to Apache raids or just simply because the caravans found a more efficient path.

---

1   A map produced in 1810 by A. Arrowsmith shows such a road running on the west side of the river from El Paso del Norte and crossing to the east side near the San Diego paraje.

A typical early supply caravan traveling the Camino probably was composed of a number of *carretas* (a two-wheeled cart with wooden wheels, pulled by a team of two to six oxen or mules), some pack mules and herds of cattle, goats, sheep, pigs and horses. There were also enough men and riding horses to operate the caravan and enough weapons to protect the cargo from possible Indian attack. The herds of animals were driven along a path separate from that taken by the people and carts. [I have been unable to find any first-hand descriptions of many of the caravans, so this description is mostly conjecture, but is based on evidence[2].] It is known that some of the early mission supply wagons were large with spoked, iron-tired wheels and were pulled by a team of 8 mules or horses. In each caravan there were typically 32 such wagons and a "large" herd of beef cattle. These caravans would make the year-and-a-half round

---

2   The trace of El Camino Real is highly evident in parts of Doña Ana County as well as other places along the route. Coronado is known to have herded the animals along their own separate path.

A typical ox-drawn carreta with wooden wheels of the type used on the El Camino Real de Tierra Adentro. Photo courtesy of Centennial Museum At the Collections, University of Texas at El Paso, Ben Wittick Collection.

A group of Carretas with spoked wheels and iron tires of a type that was probably used on the Camino Real de Tierra Adentro. These carretas were pulled by a team of two oxen as evidenced by the yoke attached to the tongue of the first carreta. Photo by Estaben Gonnet circa 1864. Public domain.

Large wagon similar to the type (but probably a later version) used to haul mission supplies along the El Camino Real de Tierra Adentro in the Spanish era through the Doña Ana paraje. Image in public domain, photographer unknown.

Another large wagon type that was likely used on the El Camino in New Mexico. These are four-wheeled wagons with the front wheels only half of the diameter of the large rear wheels. The large wheels provided less resistance on the rough and rocky trails. These wagons were pulled by eight mules harnessed abreast of each other and the hay to feed them appears to be hauled on top of the wagons. Photo by Estaben Gonnet circa 1864. Public domain.

trip from Mexico City to Santa Fe every three years[3]. On the other hand, the usual commercial caravans with their wooden-wheel carts pulled by oxen may have made a round trip every year, but some of them probably did not travel all the way from Mexico City.

The Route of El Camino Real in the Mesilla Valley and the Jornado de Muerto

The Camino Real de Tierra Adentro (also know as the Chihuahuan Trail) was used as the major route of the wagon trains hauling trade goods between Mexico City and Santa Fe for some 300 years. This period of time included about 240 years of Spanish rule, about 30 years of Mexico rule and about 30 years of USA rule over the area of New Mexico covered by

---

3   M.L. Morehead. New Mexico's Royal Road, 1958, p 33

Route of the El Camino Real de Tierra Adentro from the mission Nuestra Señora de Guadalupe in El Paso del Norte (now Juarez, Mexico) to paraje Fra Cristobal just north of the Fra Cristobal Mountains near Truth or Consequences, New Mexico. Many other parajes probably existed in the fertile Mesilla valley between the mission church and the start of the Jornado de Muerto at paraje Robledo. Modern roads are shown on the satellite image for reference.

this study. The route of the Camino was not a single trace as each wagon-master (*mayordomo*) was free to choose his own path according to prevailing conditions, the changing course of the Rio Grande and perhaps his own judgement of the possible Apache attacks. However, each caravan would have probably taken the same path whenever possible since that would not have required breaking new trail.

The route shown on the two accompanying maps indicate the main trail which stayed east of the river after the crossing near El Paso. Almost no trace of the trail is visible today in the entire Mesilla Valley from El Paso to Radium Springs due to urban development and modern farming techniques in the valley. A few short sections of the Camino can be seen on old maps and some points on the trail are known from historical accounts. The Cottonwoods paraje (known from a Butterfield Trail account), the site of Doniphan's battle in 1846 and the sites of the villages of Tortugas, Doña Ana and Radium Springs are several such known points. The short sections shown on old maps include a trail[4] marked "Road to El Paso" south of Fort Fillmore, a trail marked "Wagon Road" through the present site[5] of NMSU (New Mexico State University), the downtown portion of Mesquite Street (well known to be the Camino through common knowledge of old-timers) and the modern county road designated "Camino Real" from Las Cruces to Doña Ana. Just about the only other indication of the trail is the topographical maps of the area, a knowledge of old river beds[6,7,8] and the path of the railroad. The railroad bed is important because it was laid out (whenever possible) along slight grades which is also the same feature for which the wagon masters were searching. These hints for the route of the Camino were used to determine the path indicated on the map. From Doniphan's Brazito Battlefield the path indicated follows Highway 478 (and Doniphan Drive) into El Paso, primarily following the railroad. Even so, I think that the indicated route cannot be more than a couple of miles from the actual main route of the Camino Real de Tierra Adentro.

There apparently was another routing of the El Camino that stayed west of the river from El Paso to Mesilla where it crossed the Rio Grande and joined the main route just to the north of Las Cruces. I have found no records of any caravans that would have used this route, but it is known that the Butterfield

4   J.J. Bowden. Spanish and Mexican Land Grants, 1971, p 88
5   D. Kilcrease. A Century of Memories, 1988, Frontispiece
6   C.W. Ritter. Mesilla Comes Alive, 2014, p 47
7   See Turley map of river on page 80.
8   J.J. Bowden.. Spanish and Mexican Land Grants, 1971, p 88

The known parajes in the Mesilla Valley along the main branch of the El Camino Real de Tierra Adentro from "La Salineta" just north of El Paso, Texas to "Robledo" at Radium Springs, New Mexico shown superimposed on a modern topographical map. There was probably another branch of the camino that stayed west of the Rio Grande for most of the route to the paraje at Doña Ana. Map made with Google Earth.

Stage route went west from Fort Fillmore and met and joined a road leading north into Mesilla. Another piece of evidence of such a road to the west of the river is the Arrowsmith map of 1810 mentioned previously.

  The second of the two accompanying maps (page 21) showing the route of the Camino deals with the section of the road through the entire Jornado del Muerto from Radium Springs to the point where the trail once again meets the Rio Grande. This region is only minimally disrupted with modern highways and modern agriculture and its ninety mile length has no city developments other than the railroad town of Engle. The actual traces of the El Camino can still be seen throughout much of the this stretch of the trail, in direct contrast to the trail between El Paso and Las Cruces. Once again, we find the railroad following the older El Camino for most of the way through the Jornado de Muerto, but in this case the Camino was more dependent on routes between the natural water holes than was the railroad.

Parajes in Doña Ana County

The campgrounds (*parajes*) where the caravans spent the nights on the trail in what is now Doña Ana County (or close to it) might have numbered several dozen. It would be expected that a normal caravan operating in the later period of the Camino would be able to cover about 20 miles per day (or less if they had any trouble) so that *parajes* with water and forage might be expected at that interval for the nightly rests. But it is known that some earlier caravans traveled at a rate of about 4 miles per day and would have required *parajes* much closer together. Also, the several branches of the Camino would have required a different set of *parajes*. Today, we know the names (or approximate locations) of only a few of these rest areas.

The known *paraje* locations in Doña Ana County starting with the southern-most can be determined from the literature and are given below, along with a description of each. It should be kept in mind that various authors or travelers may apply the same name to different *parajes* or may apply different names to the same *paraje*. The following *parajes* certainly are not the only campsites along the trail, since different caravans probably traveled at different rates and traveled on different branches of El Camino Real de Tierra Adentro.

A. **Vado de los Puertos**. This ford was probably at, or near, the present location of the Santa Fe Street bridge in El Paso which is just below the narrow pass known as El Paso Canyon between the Mule Driver mountain (presently called Mount Cristo Rey) to the west and the Franklin mountains to the east. It took the Oñate expedition several days to traverse the approximately six miles through the canyon from the river crossing to the beginning of the river-bottom lands (the beginning of the Mesilla Valley) to the north of the pass. Later travelers of the Camino would bypass this "canyon" and travel to the west side of Mule Drivers Mountain. The *paraje* associated with Vado de los Puertos was probably on both sides of the Rio Grande in what is now Chihuahua, Mexico and Texas, USA. It might have taken several days to cross the river for north-bound and for south-bound caravans and it seemingly was customary to rest a night after crossing a river. The *paraje* certainly was not in Doña Ana County, but it was in both the Spanish-era and the early Mexican-era Province of New Mexico[9]. It is a natural place to start a discussion of the *parajes*.

B. **La Salineta**. This *paraje* was at a river crossing at the north end of the troublesome El Paso canyon. On one of his famous wagon caravan trips from Santa Fe to Chihuahua, Josiah Gregg[10] said they crossed the Rio Grande from east to west at the "usual place" about six miles from El Paso del Norte on September 12, 1839. He had passed by the *parajes* of Robledo and Doña Ana before the establishment of the Village of Doña Ana. Adolph Wislizenus in 1847 described its location[11] as being about six miles from El Paso del Norte (Juarez) along the route that stayed west of river and passed west of Mule Drivers Mountain. There can be little doubt the two men were describing the same crossing. It is expected to be somewhere between Doniphan Drive and the present river course along Frontera Street[12], perhaps near the Texas state line and the *paraje* could well be expected to have been close by on both sides of the Rio Grande. The site of the ford is now developed with commercial interests and modern agriculture and the river has been channelized about a mile to the west of the probable actual historic crossing site.

---

9   See the later chapter on "National Jurisdiction of the Land".
10   M.L. Morehead. Commerce on the Prairies by J. Gregg, 1954. p 272
11   A.Wislizenus. Memoir of a Tour, 1848. p 40
12   H. Jackson. Following the Royal Road, 2006. p 84

Jackson calls this site "Lower Crossing"but George D. Torok[13] calls it the "upper crossing" (but see Torok's foot note 58 for a suggestion that his name may be a misnomer, unless he meant it as a "upper" ford with respect to Vado de los Puertos). This is probably the river crossing described by Susan S. Magoffin[14] on February 15, 1847, after having spent the previous night camped about three miles from the crossing. Identifying this *paraje* as La Salineta is based on the 1810 map by A. Arrowsmith which shows that name at the proper location.

After the Indian Revolt of 1680, when the Governor of Nuevo Mexico, Antonio de Otermín, led the surviving colonists south, he stopped[15] at this *paraje*, according to George Torok (who places it somewhat north of our location), in September for about a month before continuing to El Paso del Norte. A story that Torok tells about Fr. Antonio Ayala's relief caravan for Otermín's people does not disagree with our placement of the paraje. The group of 1900 people in Otermín's party was most likely the largest group to have traveled the El Camino since the Oñate expedition.

C. **Magoffin Paraje**. Susan Magoffin said that their wagon train had camped three miles from the river crossing (presumably at La Salineta) on February 14, 1847. She did not name that *paraje*, so it might be assumed that it was just one of many places along the trail in the Mesilla Valley that was suitable for overnight camping.

D. **Canutillo**. According to Torok[16] there was a *paraje* at the present site of Canutillo, Texas which was named for a nearby cresent-shaped lake, which was probably an ox-bow lake formed by a previous course of the river. This may have been an early *paraje*, since Torok says that in the 1700s there was a military outpost here for Spanish troops from the presidio of El Paso del Norte. This site also had a settlement from 1824 to about 1830 when Apache raids chased the settlers away.

---

13   G.D. Torok. Chronicles of the Trail, 2009, Vol 5, No 2. p 7
14   S.M. Drumm. Down the Santa Fe Trail and into Mexico. p 205
15   G.D. Torok. Chronicles of the Trail, 2009, Vol 5, No 2. p 7
16   G.D. Torok. From the Pass to the Pueblos, 2012, p 119

E. **La Salinera**. Because of the similarity of its name to the one mentioned above (La Salineta) this *paraje* has been confused with the former by several writers. Torok says this site was near another ford of the river that may have been the site of a bridge in the later colonial times. Jackson identified this site (or one in its vicinity) as "La Salineta" and he says that this was the place occupied by Otermín in September and October of 1680. Jackson is probably incorrect in his identification, particularly if our conjecture about the location of La Salineta, above, is correct. This *paraje* (La Salinera) may have been the place where Susan Magoffin camped on February 13, 1847 which she called "La Laguna" and which was about 30 miles from Doña Ana. A likely location of La Laguna is now called Rainbow Lake (or the Anthony Drain) adjacent, once again, to the channelized river west of Anthony, Texas. The exact location of this *paraje* is unknown, but Edward Staski[17], a New Mexico State University archaeologist, may have discovered the remains of La Salinera in the village of Vinton, Texas about 2.5 miles south of Rainbow Lake.

F. **The Cottonwoods**. Another *paraje* (or perhaps the same *paraje*) that well fits the description of La Salineta is the place called "The Cottonwoods" that was later used as a stage stop for the Butterfield Stage Line. The site of this stage stop is well documented and is shown on the accompanying map. If the *paraje* on the Camino Real used this site, it probably covered a region that would have included what would later become the state line between Texas and New Mexico.

G. **Punto Estero Largo.** Hal Jackson mentions[18] a *paraje* at a large swamp "near Berino", NM but does not give a clue to a more exact location. Berino is located about 11 miles north of Canutillo, TX and about 5 miles north of The Cottonwoods.

H. **Brazito**. Perhaps the best description of the location of the *paraje* at Brazito is due to Susan Magoffin[19] when she wrote

---

17   E. Staski. "Some of What We Have Learned," Chronicles of the Trail, 7. 2005

18   H. Jackson. Following the Royal Road, 2006. p 79

19   S.M. Drumm.. Down the Santa Fe Trail and into Mexico. p 202

in her diary that their wagon train had "nooned" at the Brazito battlefield on February 12, 1847 the day before they camped at "La Laguna". The location of the battlefield is known to be about nine miles south of downtown Las Cruces on Highway 478. The Brazito *paraje* would be expected to be four or five miles south of the battlefield and about ten miles north of "La Laguna". The point labeled "Paraje Brazito" on the accompanying map is 5 miles from the battlefield and 10 miles from "La Laguna" and is about 1.5 miles north of Vado, NM. The actual site of the *paraje* could be reasonably within a mile of the place marked. Torok[20] mistakenly identifies a region 2.5 miles north of Vado as Doniphan's Brazito *battlefield*, but that site is quite probably the Brazito *paraje*. He does, however, state that the site was an important camping site since the early colonial period.

I. **Tortugas (La Ranchería?)**. The village of Tortugas lies just southwest of Interstate 10 across from New Mexico State University and lies along the El Camino. It is 10 miles from Paraje Brazito and is about 8.5 miles from Doña Ana and about 2 miles from downtown Las Cruces. This is likely to be the *paraje* where the Magoffin caravan stopped for the night of February 11, 1847. Susan Magoffin says they traveled 10 miles on that day, but she also implies that they got a late start leaving Doña Ana because of serious trouble caused by some of Magoffin's teamsters having stolen a cannon from the townspeople. The village of Tortugas did not come into existence until 1848 or 1849 (a year or two after the Magoffin wagon train passed though), but the site had probably been a well-used *paraje* for centuries before that. [Most of the early colonial villages sites had been sites of *parajes* because both villages and *parajes* needed fertile land.] I have not found a name for this site, but it might be the site people have called "La Ranchería" although that name might be associated with a site much closer to Las Cruces.

J. **Las Cruces (La Ranchería?)**. The town of Las Cruces was established at the same time as Tortugas and might have been at the site of "La Ranchería". This was almost certainly not the site where the Magoffin caravan spent the first night after leaving

20   G.D. Torok. Chronicles of the Trail, 2009, Vol 5, No 2. p 8

Doña Ana since it was only about 5.5 miles away whereas Susan Magoffin said that they traveled 10 miles before making camp on February 11, 1847. The actual site of "La Ranchería" is unknown but many sites in the Las Cruces / Tortugas region could have served as a *paraje*.

K. **Doña Ana**. The *paraje* at Doña Ana was probably visited by Oñate's expedition and was mentioned by name by Governor Otermín[21] in 1680 on his retreat from the Indian revolt in northern New Mexico. Although the exact location of the *paraje* has not been determined, there is evidence[22] that the modern village of Doña Ana sits on top of it. The present village of Doña Ana was first settled in 1842 and is the oldest permanent settlement in what is now southern New Mexico. For more on the village of Doña Ana, see the Chapter 6.

L. **Unnamed Paraje (Susan1)**. Susan Magoffin says that on February 7, 1847 the Magoffin wagon train camped at a place that was probably the San Diego *paraje* and that they stayed there the entire day of February 8. Their wagon train was traveling the Jornada de Muerto primarily during the night. Her diary entry for February 9 said that they traveled a "long day" and "nooned" that day at a place on the river 4 miles from the village of Doña Ana[23]. Although she did not mention passing through the *paraje* Robledo, this last statement implies that they were traveling along the Rio Grande between Robledo and Doña Ana, following the same trail as did Oñate. This unnamed place where they "nooned" on February 9 is labeled "Susan1" on the accompanying map and would have been about three-quarters of a mile northwest of Hill, NM.

M. **Paraje Robledo**. After Oñate left Paraje Doña Ana he continued going up the east bank of the Rio Grande for approximately 10 miles until he reached an *anchon* (open region) free of the thick stands of mesquite and other underbrush

---

21   G.D. Torok. From the Pass to the Pueblos, 2012, pg 136
22   Personal experience. There are charcoal remains under the foundations of buildings in the village that appear to be consistent with old campfires.
23   S.M. Drumm. Down the Santa Fe Trail and into Mexico. p 200

growing in the river bottom[24]. He stayed at the Robledo *paraje* on May 20, 1598 and at least part of May 21 when they buried Pedro Robledo (for whom the *paraje* is named). Above this site, the river runs through a narrow canyon that is unsuitable for the wagons (*carretas*) of the settlers and Oñate decided to take a small Advanced Party ahead, leaving the main part of his caravan[25] to follow him at a slower pace. This next part of the trail for the next 90 miles would later be called the "Jornado del Muerto." Paraje Robledo marks the southern end of the Jornado and is now situated in the village of Radium Springs near the ruins of Fort Selden.

N. **Unnamed Paraje (Oñate1).** Upon leaving the *paraje* Robledo, the Indian guides led the Oñate's Advance Party up an arroyo the 400 feet of elevation to the top of the plateau. They traveled only two leagues[26] (about five and a quarter miles) the first day, so probably camped close to the place labeled "Oñate1" on the accompanying map. They had to water their animals at the river which was about two and a half miles away, going down an arroyo leading from the escarpment. This is an accurate description of the location of "Oñate1". Moorhead says this campground was probably the *paraje* called "San Diego" but that site appears to be about 5.5 miles further north along the trail.

O. **San Diego Paraje**. This *paraje* lies just north of a distinctive peak called San Diego Mountain or San Diego Peak and just northwest of Detroit Tanks with its windmill that can be seen for miles around. Although Oñate probably did not use this campground, it did become one of the most used *parajes* on the Camino Real de Tierra Adentro. The site has been well documented with archaeological studies[27] and modern metal-detector hunters still occasionally find artifacts in the region. The caravans stopping at Paraje San Diego would have needed to take their livestock down one of several arroyos leading from

24   G.D. Torok. From the Pass to the Pueblos, 2012, p 141
25   M. L. Morehead. New Mexico's Royal Road, 1958, p 20
26   M. L. Morehead. New Mexico's Royal Road, 1958, p 20
27   G.D. Torok. From the Pass to the Pueblos, 2012, p 144

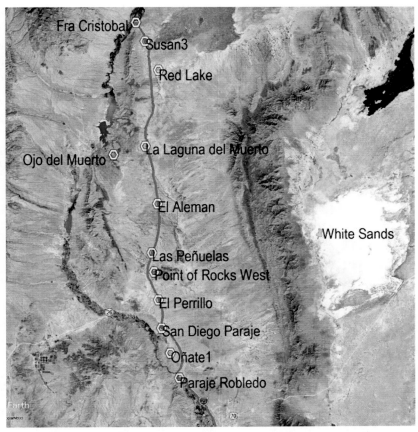

The known parajes *on the Camino Real de Tierra Adentro
along the Jornado de Muerto between paraje "Robledo" and
paraje "Fra Cristobal." The "relief" map indicates that
the trail stayed near the bottom of the drainage between the
San Andres Mountains to the east and the Caballo and Fra
Cristobal Mountains to the west in order which maximized the
chances of finding water. Modern roads are show in this view
for reference.*

the escarpment to the river below, a distance of about 2 miles.
Susan Magoffin gave a good description[28] of this paraje on
February 8 when she wrote "we camped on a high bluff about
two miles from the water, and sent the stock down to it."

28   S.M. Drumm. Down the Santa Fe Trail and into Mexico. p 200

P. **El Perrillo**. When Oñate's Advanced Party left the unnamed paraje "Oñate1" which may have been on May 22, 1598, they traveled 4 leagues (about 10.5 miles) before camping at El Perrillo (the little dog) where they found water (thanks to a dog's muddy paws, and hence the name). This means that the *paraje* El Perrillo would have been about 16 miles from the Robledo *paraje*. This would place it south of the Point of Rocks mountains in a region of many natural depressions that would catch and hold rain water after a rain. However, no one knows which depression the *perrillo* found when Oñate's Advanced Party came that way so the location of the *paraje* remains unknown.

Q. **Las Peñuelas (Oñate3)**. The second day after leaving "Oñate1" the Advanced Party left the *paraje* El Perrillo and traveling another 4 leagues they found enough water for the men in some catchments "near some volcanic rocks," probably at the place labeled "Las Peñuelas" on the accompanying map. They had to take the animals to the river which would have been about 16 miles away[29] and across the Caballo Mountains. Morehead also said that Oñate left the route that would later be called the Camino Real and headed northwest from *paraje* "Las Peñuelas" and reached an arroyo he called "Arroyo de los Muertos." The distances involved do not support that arroyo being associated with the places called Arroyo del Muerto, Ojo de los Muertos or Laguna del Muerto at the present time. I have not been able to verify Morehead's assertion that the place where Oñate abandoned the Camino (and whatever wagons he had taken with the Advanced Party) was anywhere near "Las Peñuelas." I have also not investigated his subsequent route along the river.

R. **Paraje El Alemán**. This site was named for the grave of the German, Bernardo Gruber[30], a trader running south in June 1670 in his attempted escape the from Inquisition in northern New Mexico. This site may have been visited by Oñate (if Morehead is mistaken about the location where Oñate left the route) and by the Magoffin caravan, but neither mentioned it. However,

---

29   M. L. Morehead. New Mexico's Royal Road, 1958, p 21
30   G.D. Torok. From the Pass to the Pueblos, 2012, p 149

it appears to be a well-used campsite for later travelers along the Camino Real. The site lies along the Alemán Arroyo (along the main entrance to the present Spaceport) and probably had water only during the rainy season. Unfortunately for Gruber, he passed that way during June, which is before the rainy season usually starts.

S. **Laguna del Muerto**. Almost all of the flow of traffic along the Camino Real de Tierra Adentro (including the main body of the Oñate caravan in 1598) seems to have stopped at the *paraje* of Laguna del Muerto. This lake could have been either the lake now known as "Engle Lake" or the lake immediately to the south labeled "La Laguna del Muerto" on the map. When the Magoffin wagon train stopped here on February 5, 1847 they found the lakes dry and had to go to the spring "Ojo del Muerto" about 6 miles up the arroyo to get water for themselves and their animals[31]. In her diary, Susan Magoffin says that they had come south about 29 miles from the *paraje* at Fra Cristobal and that the river (presumably at *paraje* San Diego) was another 40 miles further south. As was the custom for caravans on the Camino Real, the Magoffin train traveled primarily in the evenings and at night to avoid Apache attacks and because it was easier on the oxen and mules to travel the long periods required to make it from Fray Cristobal to San Diego in two days.

T. **Unnamed Paraje (Susan3)**. Susan Magoffin said that they camped 4 miles from Fra Cristobal on February 3 and prepared for a long trip of 25 miles to *paraje* La Laguna del Muerto. They left "Susan3" at 2:00 pm on February 4 and made it to La Laguna del Muerto at 2:00 am the next day.

U. **Paraje Fray Cristobal**. This paraje was along the Rio Grande just to the north of the Fra Cristobal Mountains. This is where the Camino Real once again meets the river at the north end of the Jornada del Muerto. It is also where Oñate and his Advanced Party re-joined the Camino Real after having traveled a route along the river west of those mountains. Paraje Fra Cristobal was used by almost all of the caravans on the Camino Real to rest both men and animals for a couple of days. For

31　S.M. Drumm. Down the Santa Fe Trail and into Mexico. p 198

those going north, the rest was necessary because their animals were exhausted coming off the Jornada de Muerto. For those going south, it was necessary to have fresh animals to survive the coming journey through the Jornada.

The above list of 21 *parajes* certainly do not represent the only campgrounds along this section of the El Camino Real and were probably not visited by every caravan. The time period that each paraje was in common use was not investigated and only a few are known to have been used by the earliest caravans.

Chapter 3
National Jurisdictions of the Land

In order to gain an understanding of the land that would eventually become the village and County of Doña Ana, it is first necessary to study the influences on that land played by Spain, Mexico, the Republic of Texas and the United States. Each had a major role in determining the history of the region.

Early Spanish Period

The region that would become known as the State of New Mexico was first discovered by Europeans in 1540 by the Coronado Expedition, but settlement was not attempted until 1598 when Oñate brought his group of colonists to the region around Santa Fe. In 1680 the Pueblo Indians revolted and were able to force out the Spanish in one of the rare occasions when any American Indians successfully resisted their invaders (but see the Suma Indian Revolt). However, the Spanish colonists came back in 1693 under the leadership of Diego de Vargas and their descendents have remained there ever since.

One of the earliest known references to the boundaries of New Mexico was made by Bishop Tamaron in 1760 while he was on an inspection tour of the northern missions. He noted that[1]

> *In the south the boundary is Carrizal, which is thirty-six leagues from El Paso. The eastern boundary is eighty leagues downstream from El Paso at the junction of the Rio Conchos.*

Bishop Tamaron does not give any other description of the boundaries which might have been due to their being ill-defined. New Mexico had been carved out of the far frontier of New Spain and there would be no need to define its boundaries specifically until there were other states in the vicinity. The approximate boundary (or perhaps, the region where the government of New Mexico exerted its influence) is shown in an accompanying map,

1   E.B. Adams. Bishop Tamaron's Visitation to New Mexico, 1954. p 192

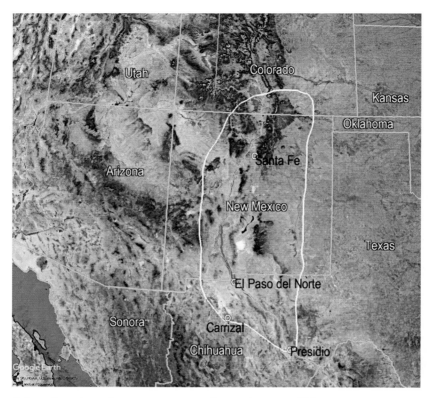

Map showing the approximate boundaries of Nuevo Mexico circa 1760 (outlined in white) and the section of the route of the El Camino Real de Tierra Adentro discussed in Chapter 2 (in center). The modern state boundaries are shown for the pertinent states in the USA and in Mexico (outlined in yellow and labeled in white). The known towns along the El Camino Real are labeled in black.

but it is unknown what the official borders might have been at the time of Bishop Tamaron's visitation.

Carrizal was a settlement about thirty miles west of the route of the El Camino but had an abundance of fresh, clear water so much of the traffic on the Camino stopped there. Carrizal had been founded in 1758, just two years before Bishop Tamaron's visit, but was probably the site of a former hacienda which had been abandoned during the Suma Indian revolt in 1684[2]. For

---

2   Full Text: El Camino Real de Tierra Adentro.. p 24

many years, Carrizal was the only town between El Paso del Norte (Juarez) and Cuidad Chihuahua.

Another of the northern frontier provinces of New Spain was the region called Texas (or Tejas) which lay along the coast of the Gulf of Mexico. It took New Spain almost two centuries to populate Texas and then only with church missions and priests. It was nearly the middle of the eighteenth century before the Canary Islanders settled around San Antonio and other settlers started to join them in populating Texas with Spaniards.

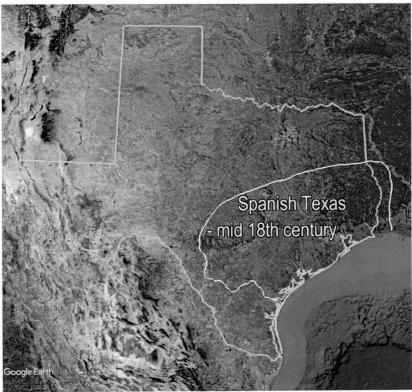

Map of approximate boundaries of Texas circa 1750. The boundaries had not been surveyed and were therefore somewhat unspecified. The information for this map is adapted from the map "Spanish Missions, Presidios, and Roads in the 17th and 18th Centuries" by the University of Texas System in 1976 which itself was adapted from a 1915 work by Herbert E. Bolton "Texas in the Middle Eighteenth Century", 1915.

About 1769, the coast of Alta California was being populated by New Spain with a chain of missions for the coastal Indians and the Presidio of San Diego was built to protect the Spanish settlers who had immigrated there. Before long, Spain had claimed the vast majority of land along the west coast of North America.

Later Spanish Period

The United States and Spain found themselves in a boundary dispute over the border between Spanish Florida and the southern States of the Union after the War of Independence from England. This dispute expanded with the purchase the Louisiana territories from France in 1803 since France and Spain had no agreement as to Louisiana's boundaries.

The uncertainty of jurisdictions extended to the provinces of New Spain as well. In his "The Exposition on the Province of New Mexico, 1812" Don Pedro Baptista Pino[3] says this about the location of Nuevo Mexico in 1811:

> From north to south New Mexico measures some 340 leagues [900 miles] and from east to west more than 350 [920 miles]. It borders Louisiana on the north along with other territories that remain unnamed. On the south by the provinces of Nueva Vizcaya, Sinaloa, and the New Kingdom of Leon. On the east by Coahuila and Texas. And to the west by the province of Sonora. I have read that it is located between the 28th and 45th degree of latitude, and the 26th and 75th degrees of longitude. But the part inhabited by the Spaniards scarcely reaches from the 36th to the 26th degree.

All of this boundary dispute was settled by a treaty negotiated by John Quincy Adams of the USA and Luis de Onís of Spain in February 1819. This treaty between the USA and Spain set the northern extent of New Spain (and New Mexico and California) at 42 degrees north latitude. The new eastern and northern boundary of New Spain after the Adams-Onís

---

3   P.B. Pino. The Exposition on the Province of New Mexico, 1812, p 7.

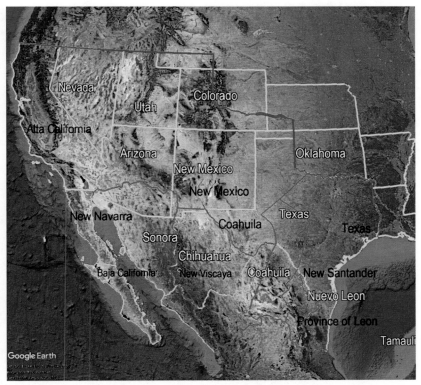

*A map showing northern New Spain as Spain was making
a treaty relinquishing its land to Mexico in 1821. The
boundaries of the Spanish states (outlined in dark with black
lettering) are approximate and are adapted from the map "The
Viceroyality of New Spain 1786 - 1821" by the University of
Texas System in 1975 which itself was adapted from a 1972
work by Enriquez Garcia de Miranda and Zaida Falcón de
Gyves in Nuevo Atlas Porrúa de República Mexicana, 1972.
The pertinent present states of the USA and of Mexico are
shown (in light outlines with white letting) for reference. The
northern boundary of New Spain extended to the Adams-Onís
line (shown in blue to the north and northeast).*

treaty of 1819 is depicted on the map on page 29 could readily be described by:

> Starting at the coast of the Gulf of Mexico at the mouth of the Sabine River, follow that river upstream to the point where it crosses the 32nd parallel of north latitude and then north to the Red River. Following the Red River upstream to the point where it meets the 100 degree of West longitude, then north to the Arkansas River. Follow the Arkansas River to its source and then north to the 42nd parallel of north latitude. Follow that parallel of north latitude to the Pacific Ocean.

Spain gave up all claims on the land north and east of the these boundaries, but Mexico had already declared its independence from Spain on September 16, 1810 and the

Adams-Onís Treaty

This treaty is the means with which Spain ceded to the USA all the land remaining in its possession in 1819 of what had been known as the region of "Florida" (extending from the Atlantic Ocean to the Mississippi River and beyond) since the time of early Spanish explorations in the sixteenth century. The USA Secretary of State John Quincy Adams and Spain's ambassador Luis de Onís signed this "Transcontinental Treaty" on February 12, 1819 in Washington, DC. This had the effect of settling the southern boundary of the of the Louisiana Purchase made by Thomas Jefferson in 1803 when the boundaries were in dispute between Spain and France some 16 years before. It also set a distinct boundary between the New Spain territories and any land that the USA might claim to the north and east of the Adams-Onís line.

The line agreed upon John Quincy Adams and Luis de Onís still forms the northern boundaries of the States of Califorinia, Nevada and Utah and forms the entire eastern boundary of the State of Texas from the panhandle to the Gulf of Mexico.

subsequent war with Mexico was not going well for Spain by 1819. Mexico won its independence in 1821, so it is probable that Spain readily accepted the Adams-Onís agreement. The new configuration of the northern part of New Spain is also shown in the accompanying map on page 29. There is no demarcation of a boundary between Spanish Provinces of Alta California and New Mexico. The population of California was almost totally along the coastline and that of New Mexico was almost totally along the Rio Grande, so there was probably no need to specify a boundary between the two.

The population of the Province of Texas was almost entirely concentrated along the Gulf coast whereas the population of Coahuila was primarily along the Rio Grande (also called the Rio Bravo). All four of these northern-most Spanish political divisions apparently were assigned political jurisdiction over very much land that was unpopulated.

Mexican Period

When Mexico won its independence from Spain in 1821, they set about writing a constitution which was finished in 1824. This constitution specified boundary changes (and name changes) to several states, combined other states and created some others. Spain ceded to Mexico all of its land south and west of the line agreed by the Adams-Onís treaty between Spain and the USA. The northern part of the resulting United States of Mexico is shown an accompanying map on page 32. For the most part, Mexico kept the boundaries that Spain had developed, including the lack of any demarcation of a boundary between the Territory of New Mexico and the Territory of Alta California. The major exception is that when the Mexican state of Chihuahua was formed out of the northern portion of New Viscaya, it took a huge portion of what had been the Spanish New Mexico from the Rio Grande in the region of the Big Bend to the southern state line of present New Mexico. What had been the Spanish Texas and Coahuila were combined under one government (the State of Coahuila y Texas), but it seems that the boundaries between the two were still recognized.

A map of the northern portion of Mexico showing the changes made by the Constitution of 1824. The Mexican states are shown in black outlines and are identified in black lettering. The boundaries are approximate and were taken from the map "Political Division of the Mexican Republic, Federal Constitution of 1824" by the University of Texas System in 1975 which itself was adapted from a 1972 work by Enriquez Garcia de Miranda and Zaida Falcón de Gyves in Nuevo Atlas Porrúa de República Mexicana, 1972. The modern US states are shown in yellow outlines and white lettering for reference.

The Republic of Texas

Spain (and later, Mexico) had claimed the land of Texas and the surrounding region since 1519 when Captain Alonso Álvarez de Peñeda mapped the coast of the Gulf of Mexico from Florida to Vera Cruz. By the mid-eighteenth century Texas was a recognized territory of Spain and had the approximate shape shown on the accompanying map of page 27. By about 1820, Spanish Texas had expanded to the north to the Red River where it remained through the Mexican Period (as it formed part of the Adams-Onís line). Spain had difficulty in populating Texas with its own citizens and opened up the region to foreigners. Moses Austin was granted some land by Spain in 1820 to settle Anglos from the United States. He died shortly thereafter and his son, Stephen F. Austin, continued with the colonization. In the meantime, of course, Mexico had won its independence from Spain and Stephen F. Austin was able to obtain a formal recognition from Mexico of the validity of his land grant. Mexico was under pressure of illegal immigration into east Texas by Anglos coming through Louisiana. Mexico also recruited colonists from several European countries and all the legal colonists were required to pledge allegiance to Mexico so that they would form a buffer against the illegal immigrants.

In 1836 the colonists of Texas revolted against Mexican rule and won their independence that same year. The Republic of Texas came into being amid a great deal of controversy about its boundaries. Mexico had considered "Texas" to be part of the State of Coahuila y Texas, but historically Coahuila, itself, had bordered on the east by the Medina River west of city of San Antonio de Bexar. The only other Mexican state bordering on the Republic of Texas was the state of Tamaulipas. Tamaulipas apparently had extended farther eastward and northeastward in 1824 but, presumably, had its border changed to the Nueces River sometime before the Texas Revolution. Mexico conceded that it had lost only Texas as they had known it, approximated by the accompanying map on page 34. However, the Republic of Texas successfully argued to set the border at the Nueces River for its full length, thereby taking the eastern portion of the state

*The approximate boundaries of the southwestern
part of Texas showing the probable extent of the land which
Mexico ceded to Texas after the Texan Revolution of 1835. The
Mexican states are outlined in red and the Rio Grande is shown
in blue for reference (although it did not form the border of any
Mexican state at the time). This would have kept the Medina
River as the eastern border of Coahuila and the Nueces River
as the northeastern border of Tamaulipas as had been the
traditional boundaries of the Mexican states.*

of Coahuila. This boundary apparently became the *de facto*
border of the Republic of Texas that was accepted by Mexico
and later by the USA.

However, the Republic of Texas almost immediately laid
claim to all of the land east and north of the Rio Grande from its
mouth on the Gulf of Mexico to its headwaters in what would
become the state of Colorado and from that point northward to
the 42nd parallel of latitude. It is this claim that includes the

region which would become known as Doña Ana and which makes Texas pertinent to our present study. The final version of the Republic of Texas along with its new claims are shown in the map on this page. Mexico never recognized Texas's claim of the Rio Grande as its border with Mexico. The final configuration of the State of Texas would not be resolved until Texas became a part of the USA and until the United States went to war with Mexico to decide Texas' claims as well as the fate of much of the rest of Mexico's land in what is now the United States. In the meantime, Mexico maintained sovereignty over the land of New Mexico, albeit the southern part of that land (up to the latitude of

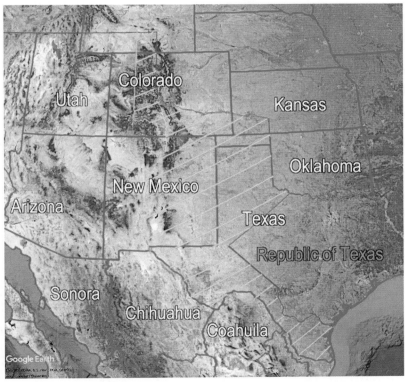

Texas after the Revolution. The Republic of Texas (approximated here in red outline) was accepted by Mexico, but Texas' claim of the land east of the Rio Grande and extending to the Adams-Onís line (shown here by yellow hatch marks) was never recognized by Mexico.

San Diego Peak or the southern end of the Jornado del Muerto) had been assigned to the state of Chihuahua. The government of Chihuahua made several land grants in that region during the period of 1836 and 1846 (i.e., when Texas was a Republic but before Texas became a state of the USA).

A note about the boundary lines as drawn in the maps in this section is in order. Much of the information that is readily available about the boundaries of Texas at different periods of time is available in the literature in the form of maps. However, even the best mapmakers seem to have taken liberal "artistic license" in drawing their boundaries. The best resulting boundaries as I have drawn them may still be several tens of miles out of place, and may be even worse where the boundaries are not specified by rivers or by international treaties. In all cases, I have characterized the borders as "approximate" and they should be taken to represent only "reasonable guesses" to the actual borders.

United State of America

When Texas became a state on December 29, 1845 it was admitted to the union without its boundaries being specified. Texas' claim of the Rio Grande as a boundary had not yet been resolved and Mexico severed diplomatic ties with the USA over that issue. Talks between the two nations eventually failed and the US declared war on Mexico in May of 1846 and Mexico declared war on the US in July of 1846. By that date, General Stephen Watts Kearney had already taken command of the Army of the West with orders to take New Mexico and California. Gen. Kearney captured the Capital of New Mexico, Santa Fe, without a shot being fired. Kearney then sent Col. Alexander William Doniphan south from Santa Fe to Chihuahua City. Doniphan had been joined by James Kirker and his band of scalp hunters at the Brazito Battlefield, a short day's travel from the village of Doña Ana, just after Doniphan's battle against Mexican troops from El Paso del Norte.

By the time the war between the US and Mexico was over in 1848, the US had captured Chihuahua and Mexico City and had maintained two separate fronts, one in California and one in the interior of Mexico, for about two years. As a result of the war, Mexico gave up all land north and east of the Rio Grande, the claim to which had been inherited by the USA with the annexation of Texas. But perhaps even more important, Mexico also lost all the land west of the Rio Grande and south of the Adams-Onís treaty line that was not covered by Texas' claim. This latter loss of land includes the present states of California, Nevada and Utah and the bulk of Arizona and New Mexico and a significant portion of Colorado and Wyoming. Mexico lost about half of its land to the USA as a result of the war as can be seen on the accompanying map on this page. The southern border of the USA was not surveyed until several years later when the Bartlett-García Conde (see sidebar on page 41) survey was completed and can be described as:

> Starting with the first point of the survey near the village of Doña Ana where the Rio Grande meets with latitude 32° 22' and going west for 3° of longitude and then due

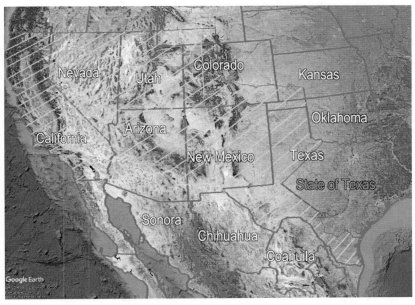

Land lost by Mexico (and gained by the USA) as a direct result of the War with Mexico between 1846 and 1848 (shown with yellow hatch marks).

north to meet with the Gila River. Following that river to it's confluence with the Colorado River at Yuma and then going due west to the Pacific Ocean.

With the end of the war, some settlers from Doña Ana, and other places, started a settlement at Mesilla on the west side of the river (and below the 32° 22' parallel of latitude) where they could maintain their Mexican citizenship. But even before the Bartlett-García Conde survey was completed, many people in the US were dissatisfied with it because it had neglected to include a reasonable route for a railroad to the north of the new border. Others were dissatisfied because it did not include the western part of the Mesilla Valley and its fertile land. To rectify this situation, the USA entered into an agreement with Mexico in 1854 to buy some land south of the Gila River in what came to be known as the Gadsden Purchase. The Gadsden Purchase extended from the Bartlett - Garcia Conde line in the north, southward along the Rio Grande to a southern line described[4] as:

---

4   S. R. DeLong. The History of Arizona, 1905. p 14.

The Gadsden Purchase (shown as red hatching)
completed the present border between Mexico and the USA.

*Commencing at a point in the center of the Rio Grande,
north latitude 31 ° 37', thence west one hundred miles;
thence south to north latitude 31 ° 20' ; thence west to
111° meridian west from Greenwich ; thence to a point
in the center of the Colorado River, twenty miles below
the mouth of the Gila River ; thence up the Colorado to
southeast corner of the State of California.*

This, of course, resulted in the village of Mesilla being part of
the USA, but most of the settlers stayed, anyway. This boundary
established by the Gadsden Purchase is still recognized to this
day and is indicated on an accompanying map on page 38.

The USA assigned to Texas all of the land east and north
of the Rio Grande, south of the 32nd parallel of latitude and
east of the 103° of West Longitude (or close to that, because of
surveyor's errors[5]) with the Compromise of 1850. This fixed

5   M. Baker. Northwest Boundary of Texas, 1902.

*The extent of Doña Ana County in the Territory of
New Mexico after the Gadsden Purchase of 1854. Doña Ana
County and the Territory of New Mexico were established
in 1852, but the western portion of the county did not get
appended until 1854.*

the state lines of Texas at their present locations and thereby fixed the eastern "state line" of the New Mexico Territory.

With the completion of the Gadsden Purchase, the added land was assigned to Doña Ana County which resulted in that county's stretching from the western state line of Texas (at longitude approximately 103° West) to the mouth of the Gila River at the California state line (California had been admitted as a state of the USA in 1850). The northern boundary of Doña Ana county followed the 33rd parallel of latitude (approximately) to the Gila River and then followed the Gila to the California state line as depicted in the map on page 39. The Territory of New Mexico extended from the Arkansas River near Bent's Fort in the north to latitude 31° 20' (the border with Mexico after the Gadsden Purchase) in the south.

Confederate States of America

When the Texas Confederate forces of Lt. John Baylor occupied the village of Mesilla on July 25, 1861 it was the first act of aggression by the Confederate States of America (CSA) in New Mexico. After Baylor's troops defeated Major Isaac Lynde's force from Fort Fillmore at San Augustine Springs in the Organ Mountains on July 27, Baylor reorganized the southern part of the US Territory of New Mexico into the Confederate Territory of Arizona with Mesilla as its capital. The Confederate Territory of Arizona extended[6] from the border with Mexico and the state line of Texas in the south to the latitude of 34 degrees to the north, incorporating the southern portion of the present states of New Mexico and Arizona. The Territory of Arizona was the only Territory in the Confederate State of America.

General Henry Hopkins Sibley mounted a full scale Confederate invasion[7] of New Mexico in early 1862 with the presumed intention of capturing the gold fields of Colorado. Sibley defeated the US troops from Ft. Craig at Valverde on February 21, 1862 and went on to capture Albuquerque and Santa Fe before being defeated and losing his supply wagon train on

---

6   Beck and Haase, Historical Atlas of New Mexico, 1969. p 31.
7   R. Wadsworth. Forgotten Fortress, 2002, p 335.

March 29 at Glorieta Pass. After that defeat, the Confederates retreated back south, but the advancing California Column of Gen. James Carleton forced the Confederates to continue their retreat to El Paso and eventually to Ft. Davis. This ended the Confederate Territory of Arizona and the role of Mesilla as the capital city. The Confederate occupation of New Mexico lasted for about nine months.

United State of America (again)

After the Confederates vacated the southern part of New Mexico, all of the Territory of New Mexico once again came under control of the USA. In 1867 Congress created the Territory of Arizona out of the western part of the Territory of New Mexico starting at the 109° 3' of West Longitude (i.e. starting at 32° west of the observatory at Washington, DC) and extending to the California state line. When Colorado became a State in 1876, it was granted the part of New Mexico Territory north of the 37th parallel of North Latitude. What was left of the Territory of New Mexico eventually became a State of the US in 1912.

Confusion of the Bartlett-García Conde Name.

To avoid some possible confusion, it is well to keep in mind that the name applied to much of the border controversy is that of two men: John Russel Bartlett, the US representative to the Boundary Commission, and Pedro García Conde, the Mexico representative. García Conde has a double last name which is sometimes hyphenated.

It is also well to keep in mind that Pedro García Conde is a different person from Francisco García Conde, the Governor of Chihuahua from 1840 to 1842.

42   *Doña Ana*

Chapter 4

Early European Settlements in Southern New Mexico and Doña Ana County

Several pueblo Indian settlements existed at the time of the first European exploration of the region of interest in this chapter, but most seem to have disappeared within two or three generations. This may have been the result of European diseases[1] on the indigenous population or, perhaps, by the territory take-over by the Apaches. In any case, the Apache dominance of this entire land occurred in a relatively short period of time and lasted until 1880 when Chief Victorio was killed by the Mexicans at Tres Castillos. Geronimo soon surrendered to the US Army in 1886 which essentially ended the Apache resistance.

During the periods of the Spanish and the Mexican jurisdictions, land grants[2] were issued in three distinct categories:

1. *Colony*: A group of citizens or perhaps an individual representing the group was granted land with the stipulation that the group relocated to the land to live. They were to make certain improvements and to defend the colony against Indian attacks.

2. *Empresario*: An individual was granted land for the purpose of attracting foreign people to settle and work the land. The individual settlers were required to become citizens of Spain or Mexico.

3. *Individual*: An individual was granted land in his own name, usually for the purpose of ranching or mining, probably, but perhaps also for the Church missions. Some of these grants may have developed colonies of settlers or farmers, but apparently the land still belonged to the individual grantee.

In this chapter, we will be concerned with only the European (primarily Spanish, Mexican and US) settlements that

---

1 D.T. Reff. Depopulation and Culture Change 1518-1764, 1991.
2 J.J. Bowden. Spanish and Mexican Land Grants, 1971. pg 3

occurred in the early part of the European occupation up to about 1848, the end of the Mexican War. Specifically, this chapter will not deal with;

- the Spanish Mission Churches,

- the ranches or haciendas that belonged to Spanish individuals and which seem to have been scattered throughout the region, nor

- the *presidios* (military forts) that were established to protect the settlers, the individual ranches, the Church missions and the other interests of the government which had jurisdiction over the region at various times.

Settlements in the Chihuahuan part of New Mexico

A. *El Carrizal*:

The settlement of El Carrizal marked the southern boundary of New Mexico until about the time of Mexico's independence from Spain in 1820. It was a settlement about 80 miles south of El Paso del Norte and about thirty miles west of the route of the El Camino Real de Tierra Adentro but had an abundance of fresh, clear water so much of the traffic on the Camino stopped there. Carrizal had been founded in 1758, just two years before Bishop Tamaron paid a visit to that[3] local church. This site was probably the site of a former hacienda which had been abandoned during the Suma Indian revolt in 1684[4].

B. *El Paso del Norte*:

Ever since Oñate led his settlers to northern New Mexico in 1598, El Paso del Norte had been an important *paraje* on the Camino Real in what was then still part of New Mexico. There has been a Spanish presence around the present city of Juarez, Mexico (then called El Paso del Norte) since 1659 when Fray García de San Francisco established Nuestra Señora de Guadalupe Mission. But it was not until 1682 when Oñate's settler's descendants were forced south out of northern New

---

3   E.B.Adams. Bishop Tamaron's Visitation to New Mexico, 1954. p 192
4   Full Text: El Camino Real.de Tierra Adentro. pg 24

Mexico by the Pueblo Revolt that the region around El Paso del Norte gained European residents (other than the missionary priests). The Spanish colonists and their Indian allies were led by Gov. Otermín to the area around the Guadalupe Mission and established five settlements close by: one of which they called El Paso del Norte surrounding the mission and four others a bit further away, San Lorenzo, Senecú, Ysleta and Socorro[5]. The population of these towns represent a continuous peopling of the region to the present time. This population also supplied the 900 men, women and children that Diego de Vargas took with him to resettle northern New Mexico in 1693.

Settlements in the Doña Ana County part of New Mexico

A. John Heath (Juan Gid) Colony Grant:

The only land grant made under the Empresario system in this region was one made to John Heath (also known by his Spanish name, Juan Gid) in the El Brazito area of the Mesilla Valley. On December 27, 1822 Heath had petitioned the Emperor of Mexico, Austín de Iturbide, for 25 leagues of land that had been claimed by Juan Antonio Garcia under an Individual land grant. Garcia had been forced to abandon the land in 1821 because of Indian uprisings while his petition was still pending. On January 4, 1823 the Mexico General Assembly had passed a new colonization law, and Heath was notified that his previous petition would not acted upon. On the same day, April 3, 1823, Heath submitted another petition and the 25 leagues at El Brazito was granted on that same day, also. But with the stipulation that the grant be approved by the Governor of New Mexico in Santa Fe.

Upon receiving the land grant, Heath returned to Missouri to get the 30 families he had promised for the colony and all the equipment and supplies needed to begin the settlement at El Brazito. But when the settlers arrived at the site of the colony they learned that the Government of New Mexico and the

5   http://www.tshaonline.org/handbook/online/articles/hdelu. Acc. 6/23/2019

Assembly had repudiated the issuance of the grant and they were shortly ordered off the land. This was probably the shortest-lived colony in the history of Doña Ana County.

B. The Doña Ana Bend Colony Grant:

1. The Village of Doña Ana

On September 18, 1839 a group of 116 citizens (presumably counting only men, as was the custom) of El Paso del Norte under the leadership of José María Costales began the process of applying for lands to colonize at the *paraje* of Doña Ana. Parts of land they petitioned had twice before been granted to someone else almost twenty years prior (Juan Antonio Garcia and John Heath) but both lost their grants for various reasons. Their petition was approved by Governor J. María Yrigoyen of the State of Chihuahua on October 18, 1839 and was approved by the Chihuahuan State Assembly on December 5, 1839. However, no further action was taken at that time, so on July 3, 1840 the colonists started the process over again under the new Governor, Francisco García Conde. Conde approved the new petition on July 8, 1840 and ordered the establishment of the colony on August 5, 1840[6].

Due to Apache uprisings, the colonists were not able to go to the Doña Ana Bend at that time and requested - and were granted - permission to delay moving to the colony until February 1, 1843. On January 26, 1843, 33 men of the original 116 colonists notified the authorities and immediately began to move to the colony. But the Apaches again turned hostile and by April 16, 1843 only 14 settlers remained[7,8] at the Doña Ana Bend Colony Grant.

Much more detailed information on the Doña Ana Bend Colony Grant will be found in the subsequent chapters entitled "Doña Ana Bend Colony Grant" and "Doña Ana Village."

---

6   J.J. Bowden. Spanish and Mexican Land Grants, 1971. p 67

7   M.E. McFie. A History of the Mesilla Valley - 1903, 1999. p. 16.

8   Doña Ana Historical 2019 Calendar.

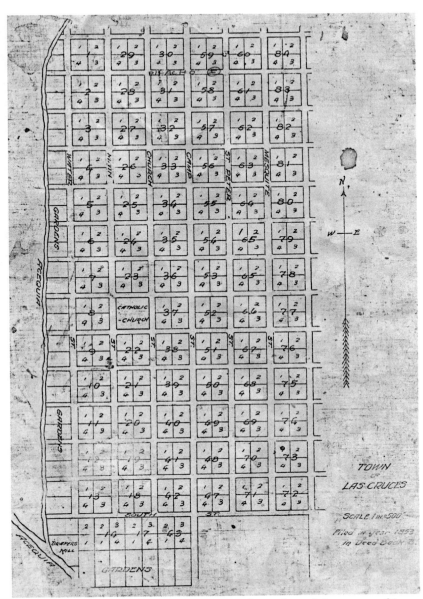

An 1853 copy of the original 1849 Sackett plat of the town of Las Cruces showing the numbered 84 blocks and the unnumbered block for the plaza and church. Title: "Town of Las Cruces, Scale 1 in. = 500', Filed in year 1853 in Deed Book 2." The Donald H. Wiese survey records. Ms0463. New Mexico State University Library, Archives and Special Collections.

2. Las Cruces

By the time the US Dragoons established a post at Doña Ana in 1848, there was sufficient pressure, both social and political, to warrant the development of another village. Lt. Delos Bennett Sackett[9] (in temporary command of the post at Doña Ana) agreed to lay out the Village of Las Cruces in 1849 at the request[10] of Pedro Melendres. Sackett may have assigned the job to another officer (named Chapman according to Maude McFie, p 40) and perhaps five other men, including Charles Henry Coleman[11] and George Achenback[12]. The town these men surveyed had 84 blocks plus one block they specified was to be for the plaza and church. The plat of this town is presented in the graphic on the previous page. Each of the 84 blocks was divided into four equal individual lots, but one of these blocks (No. 53 between Campo Street and San Pedro Street and Court Ave and Las Cruces Ave) was designated as the cemetery (or camposanto). Only 28 blocks (bounded by Water Street on the west, by San Pedro Street on the east, by Augustine Ave on the north and by Griggs Ave on the south) were allotted to the original settlers. There would have been 26 blocks (or a maximum of 104 lots), excluding the camposanto and plaza/church blocks, to be allotted to heads of families of the original 120[13] settlers of Las Cruces by drawing lot numbers from a hat.

At the present time, we do not know how many "heads of families" there were at the drawing nor what their names may have been. However, one of the early plat maps (presented in an accompanying graphic) has names penciled-in on some of the lots. This map is presented on the following page and larger-scale excerpts are included in the following three figures. This plat is labeled as being from 1853 but has street names penciled-in that appear to be after 1870. For instance, the street labeled "South St." in the Sackett plat is labeled "Convent" in this map,

9   W. S. Kiser. Dragoons in Apacheland, 2012. p 64.
10   M. E. McFie. A History of the Mesilla Valley, 1903. p 60 n2
11   Doña Ana Historical 2017 Calendar. .
12   M. E. McFie. A History of the Mesilla Valley, 1903. p 60 n2
13   G. Owen. Multicultural Crossroads, 2005. p 30.

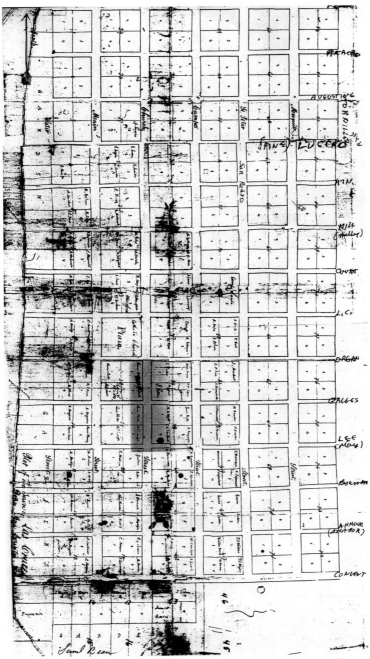

Documentation for list of original settlers. Rio Grande Historical Information File (CCF)-Las Cruces Plot of Town, 1853. New Mexico State University Library, Archives and Special Collections.

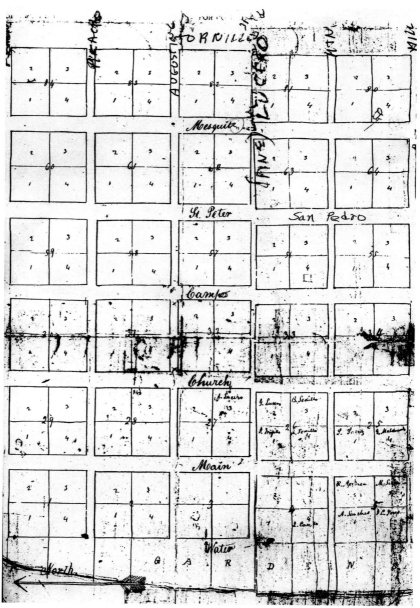

Detail of "Document for list of original settlers": North Part of Las Cruces. East is toward the top of page. Rio Grande Historical Information File (CCF)-Las Cruces Plot of Town, 1853. New Mexico State University Library, Archives and Special Collections.

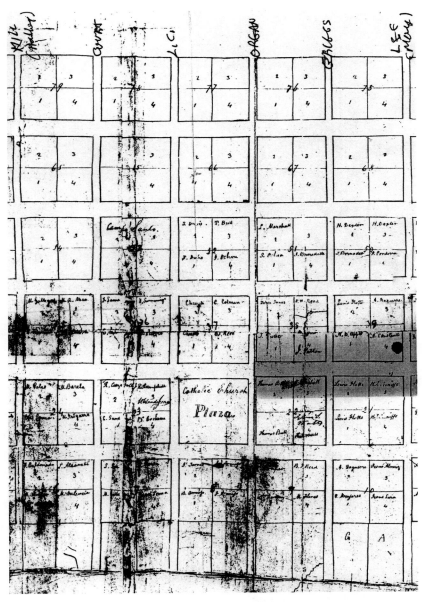

Detail of "Document for list of original settlers": Middle Part of Las Cruces. East is toward the top of page. Rio Grande Historical Information File (CCF)-Las Cruces Plot of Town, 1853. New Mexico State University Library, Archives and Special Collections.

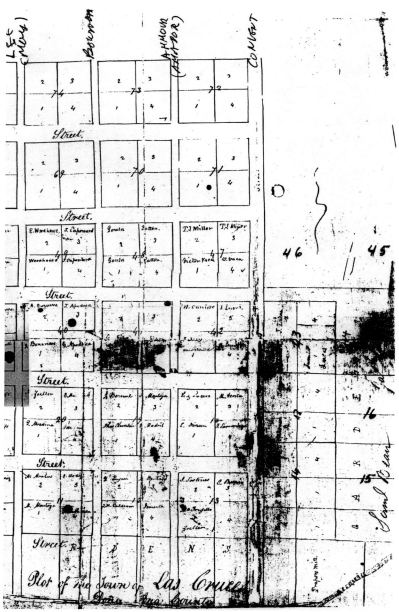

Detail of "Document for list of original settlers": South Part of Las Cruces. East is toward the top of page. Rio Grande Historical Information File (CCF)-Las Cruces Plot of Town, 1853. New Mexico State University Library, Archives and Special Collections.

Name	First Names	Bloc	Lot	Name	First Names	Bloc	Lot
				Table 4.1 Early Settlers of Las Cruces			
Acoma	M.	18	3	Chursk (?) Church?	none	37	2
Aldarebe (?)	L.	6	3	Cochran	P. S. (?)	23	4
Alvarez	Jesus	10	3	Colman (Coleman?)	C(harles Henry	37	3
Apodaca	J.	40	3	Constanti	A.	39	4
Apodaca	R.	5	2	Cordova	I. (?)	50	4
Apodaca	Y.(?)	40	4	Cuniffe	H.	21	3
Apple	N. B.	39	1	Cuniffe	H.	21	4
Armijo	(?)	8	3	Cuniffe	H.	42	2
Armijo	B.	8	1	Cuniffe (?)	H. (?)	42	4
Armijo	F. (?)	8	4	Davis (Duvis?)	F. (?)	52	1
Avalos (?)	A.	11	2	Davis (Duvis?)	J.	52	2
Baldanado	F. (?)	6	2	Dexter	H.	50	2
Barela	M. (?)	24	3	Dexter	H.	50	3
Barrio	C.	13	3	Draper	Draper's Mill	x	x
Bean	Samuel G.	15	1	Dugan (?)	M. (?)	6	1
Bean	Samuel G.	15	2	Duguerre	A.	40	2
Bean	Samuel G.	15	3	Durun (Duran?)	E.	18	1
Bean	Samuel G.	15	4	Finly (?)	(?)	42	1
Bean	Samuel G.	16	1	Flores	M.	9	4
Bean	Samuel G.	16	2	Flotte (?)	Lewis	21	1
Bean	Samuel G.	x	1	Flotte (?)	Lewis	21	2
Bean	Samuel G.	x	2	Flotte (?)	Lewis	39	2
Benavides	I. (?)	40	1	Friez (?)	L.	25	1
Bernadet	J.	50	1	Frigarre	U. (?)	24	4
Bernal	L.	19	2	Gaguerre (?)	A. (?)	10	2
Bernatte	I. (?)	51	4	Gaguerre (?)	A. (?)	39	3
Bonfier (?)	(?)	9	2	Gallegos (?)	M.	35	2
Bull	T.	52	3	Jones	John	38	2
Bull	Thomas	22	1	Jones (?)	J(ohn) C.	5	4
Bull	Thomas	22	2	Jotla (?)	M.	7	1
Calderon	J. M.(?)	12	1	Lama	Jesus	7	4
Campbell	C. (?)	22	3	Lama	L. (?)	36	2
Campbell	R.	23	2	Lama	Plas (?)	24	1
Capoulara (?)	J.	49	3	Lara	Jesus	10	4
Capoulara (?)	J.	49	4	Liuet (?)	(?)	41	4
Carillo (?)	L.	4	4	Lucas	J.	43	3
Churrton	(?)	19	1	Lucas (?)	I. (?)	42	3
Chursk (?) Church?	none	37	1	Lucas (?)	J.	43	1

x signifies an un-numbered block/lot. ? Signifies unknown Information.

A listing heads of households of some of the early settlers of Las Cruces circa 1853. This listing of names is probably incomplete and has misspellings due to difficulty in reading the hand written notations on the available photocopy of the original document. Question marks in this chart indicates data that is unknown. This list may contain names of individuals who came to Las Cruces considerably later than 1853.

Name	First Names	Block	Lot	Name	First Names	Block	Lot
				Table 4.1 Early Settlers of Las Cruces (continued)			
Lucero	A.	27	3	Sanchez	A.	5	1
Lucero	Luz	18	2	Sand	C.	23	1
Lucero	S. (?)	36	4	Sax (?)	S. (?)	7	2
Lucero	Y.	26	2	Sedillo	A. (?)	26	4
Lujan	Y.(?)	12	2	Sedillo	B.	26	3
Madrid				Serna (?)	M.	5	3
Madrid (?)	J. (?)	19	4	Sila (?)	C.	41	1
Maldonado	Y. (?)	25	4	Sostines	I. (?)	13	2
Marshall	L.	51	2	Soula	(?)	48	1
Me(?)	D.	20	3	Soula	(?)	48	2
Medina	P.	20	1	Torres	I. (?)	8	2
Miller	T.J.	47	2	Trujillo	L. (?)	14	2
Miller	T.J.	47	3	Trujillo	L. (?)	x	2
Minjares	(?)	10	1	Trujillo	M. (?)	13	1
Montano (?)	(?)	12	3	Trujillo	Y. (?)	26	1
Montoya	(?)	19	3	Tucker	J.	38	1
Montoya	M.	11	1	Tucker	P. H.	?	?
Ochoa	I. (?)	52	4	Vaca	M. A.	35	3
Ochoa	S.	51	1	Vaca	Victor	47	1
Ochoa	S.	52	4	Vaca	Victor	47	4
Olguin	J.	17	3	Valencia	M.	6	4
Ortiz	S. (?)	11	3	Wandefine (?)	W. (?)	23	3
Padilla	S. (?)	11	4	Watts	(?) L.	22	4
Patton	(?)	48	3	Woodhouse	E.	49	2
Patton	(?)	48	4	Woodhouse	E. (?)	49	1
Patton	L. (?)	38	4	Zoeller	A.	20	2
Poles	M.	24	2	(?)	(?)	43	2
Reed	B. F.	9	3	(?)	Joe	20	4
Reed	J. M.	38	3	(?)	L. (?)	7	3
Reed	OF. (?)	37	4	(?)	S.	14	3
Robinson (?)	C. W.	17	2	(?)	T. (?)	9	1
S(F)ementa	(?)	12	4	(?)	?	35	1
Samaniego	E. (?)	36	3	(?)	?	35	4
Samaniego	F.	18	4	(?)	?	36	1

x signifies an un-numbered block/lot. ? Signifies unknown Information.

but the Sisters of Loretto did not start their school[14] (or convent) until January 7, 1870. That street is now called "Lohman Avenue". Also at least one man named on the map, Samuel Bean, is known to have come to Las Cruces sometime after 1861 when his business interests in Pinos Altos dried up. However, it is entirely possible that Sam Bean was in Las Cruces very close to 1849 soon after he married the daughter of James Kirker in El Paso del Norte. Another possible hint that the information on the plat does not date from 1849 is the name of "Woodhouse"

14   R. Buchanan. The First 100 Years, 1961. p 67.

on block 49, lots 1 and 2. Lot 2 is labeled "E. Woodhouse" but if either of these two lots belonged to Dr. S. W. Woodhouse he could not have acquired the lot before he came to town[15] in the June 1851.

Presuming that the names on the plat represent the individuals who drew those lots from the hat in 1849 appears to be wholly unjustified, but it does provide some insight into the first decade or two of the life of the town. Table 4.1 lists the names of 106 men which are discernible today. In addition I count six more men who owned lots but whose name cannot be deciphered. In all, the 1853 map indicates that 114 men owned 140 lots in town, but we do not know precisely when that was, nor do we know if they all held the lots at the same time.

3. Tortugas

The village of Tortugas may have been surveyed as early as 1849 at the same time (or very close to it) and perhaps by the same men who surveyed Las Cruces. This village was probably called "San Juan" when it was first started and occupied only the northern part of the present-day village. In February 1852 it was noted[16] that "Tortugas Pueblo" was one of the populated places between El Paso del Norte and Las Cruces. However, on the map he published in 1854 for Captain J. Pope, Lt. K. Carrard lists "Las Tortugas" as being founded in 1852 and having a population of 100 in 1854.

4. San Ysidro

San Ysidro is a small farming village about 2.5 miles south of Doña Ana and about 3.5 miles north of Las Cruces just west of the present railroad tracks. It is situated within the Doña Ana Bend Colony Grant. Most of what is known about the early history of San Ysidro is due to its inclusion in the book *Our Heritage Our People* by Ella Banegas Curry and Shan Nichols. As part of her Banegas family's story, Ella Banegas Curry says her grandfather, Manuel Banegas, was one of the early settlers of the village and her family still lives in the vicinity today. She

---

15   W. S. Kiser. Dragoons in Apacheland, 2012. p 64.
16   R. Wadsworth. Forgotten Fortress, 2002. p 65.

says that her father, Estevan Banegas (one of Manuel's sons), donated the land when the church was built in 1922 "about seventy-five years after the village had been settled[17]." This would imply that the village was settled in 1847 and would pre-date both Las Curces and Tortugas. There is no "Banegas" listed in any of the lists of early settlers of the Doña Ana Bend Colony Grant (see the lists in Chapter 6) so it would seem that Manuel Banegas must have come to the region sometime after 1843. He certainly could have been allotted farm land in the Doña Ana Bend Colony Grant at the time. See Chapter 6 for the conditions for later settlers to obtain farm land.

C. Mesilla Civil Colony Grant

La Mesilla was surveyed in March or April of 1851 according to Thomas Bull[18] who moved there about that time, along with other US citizens, believing that west side of the Rio Grande was part of the United States. [Thomas Bull also had three lots in the town of Las Cruces on the 1853 map of that town. Bull moved to Las Cruces as soon as he learned that La Mesilla had been effectively ceded to Mexico by Bartlett and the Boundary Commission.] At about the same time as Thomas Bull arrived in La Mesilla, Rafael Ruelas had lead a group of settlers[19] from the village of Doña Ana to La Mesilla, believing that it was part of Mexico. The confusion as to which nation the region of La Mesilla belonged was due to two factors. The first factor is the gross mistakes on the map made by John Disturnell map of 1846 and the second factor is the Treaty of Guadulupe Hidalgo which specified the border between Mexico and the US to extend west from a point near El Paso del Norte. Everyone (except, perhaps, John Disturnell) knew where El Paso del Norte was located, but when the US border commissioner Bartlett agreed to place the border at 32° 22' North Latitude (several miles north of La Mesilla) he brought the entire region west of the Rio Grande between El Paso and the Doña Ana into a "disputed" status.

---

17   Curry and Nichols. Our Heritage Our People, 1974. p53.
18   D. Thomas. La Posta, 2013. pp 8, 9.
19   C. W. Ritter. Mesilla Comes Alive, 2014. p 70.

This issue would not be settled until 1854 when the Gadsden Purchase agreement was ratified by both Mexico and the US. In the meantime, the Mexican State of Chihuahua once again assumed jurisdiction of the lands around La Mesilla. It was the Chihuahua General Commissioner of Emigration, Ramón Ortiz, who officially[20] established the Mesilla and Santo Tomás Civil Colony Grant on January 20, 1852 (see also the next entry "Santo Tomás, below) and began distributing[21] land to Ruelas' colonists by sometime in August 1851.

Ramón Ortiz divided the land of the Colony into an unspecified number of agricultural lots measuring 960 varas by 960 varas (or about 160 acres). (See Appendix 1 for a definition of "vara" and other measures used the mid-nineteenth century and their modern equivalents.) He may have distributed some of these 160 acre lots to Rafael Ruelas and some of his original settlers from Doña Ana, but he soon found it necessary to divide his original lots by a factor of three. Each lots would have been about 960 varas by 320 varas (or about 53.3 acres). Apparently before he was finished distributing the farming lots, Ortiz had further reduced allotments[22] to about 25 acres or less. Where the individual lots were located and to whom each was distributed is unknown.

Also unknown is the layout or plat of the town lots and which individual family or individual person received each of those lots. It is known that Ramón Ortiz had distributed both the agricultural lots and the town lots to the original settlers before he officially founded the Colony on January 20, 1852, so there may be some hope that such information will eventually surface.

According to C. W. Ritter's book[23] "Mesilla Comes Alive", the 1850 census (presumably a US census) showed a population of 700 at La Mesilla. The Mexican census of December 1851 indicates a population of La Mesilla of 1230 individuals. The 1854 Carrard (or Pope) map of the Mesilla

---

20   J.J. Bowden. Spanish and Mexican Land Grants, 1971. p 40.
21   D. Thomas. La Posta, 2013. pp 8, 9.
22   D. Thomas. La Posta, 2013. pp 8, 9.
23   C. W. Ritter. Mesilla Comes Alive, 2014. p 70.

Valley indicates a population of 3,000 in La Mesilla whereas the populations of Doña Ana and Las Cruces had shrunk to 600 individuals, each.

D. Santo Tomás

Santo Tomás was first settled along with La Mesilla in 1850, but it was too close to La Mesilla for Commissioner Ortiz to consider making it a separate colony. He incorporated both into the Mesilla and Santo Tomás Civil Colony Grant, but before the official paperwork was completed, Ortiz was replaced with Guadalupe Miranda early in 1853. Miranda divided Ortiz's original Mesilla Grant into the Mesilla Civil Colony Grant and the Santo Tomás de Yturbide Grant on August 3[24], 1853.

In his map of 1854, Lt. K. Carrard lists "San Tomas" as having a population of 300 and having been first settled in 1852. This agrees with our findings about the founding of La Mesilla. See also Appendix 2.

E. Picacho

Commissioner Miranda recommended[25] the establishment of the settlement of Picacho because of the large population of La Mesilla and he intended to move some of that population to the new settlement. Picacho is located on the west side of the Rio Grande at the foot of Picacho Peak about three miles south of the Bartlett-García Conde Compromise border line of 32° 22' North Latitude. The village of Picacho was therefore included in the Gadsden Purchase of 1854. Miranda's recommendation may have been made during his August 3, 1853 breakup of the Mesilla Colony Grant, but the first settlement at Picacho apparently did not happen until about 1855[26].

Settlements in the Arizona part of New Mexico

A. Tubac:

Tubac was established in 1752 as a Spanish *presidio*[27] along the Santa Cruz river in a region the Spanish called the

24   J.J. Bowden. Spanish and Mexican Land Grants, 1971. p 40.
25   J.J. Bowden. Spanish and Mexican Land Grants, 1971. p 50.
26   Curry and Nichols. Our Heritage, Our People. 1974. p 75.
27   http://en.wikipedia.org/wiki/Tubac,_Arizona. Acc 6/26/2019

Pimería Alta and which, after the Gadsden Purchase, became part of Doña Ana County, New Mexico Territory and which is now part of the State of Arizona. In addition to the soldiers at the presidio, there apparently was a colony of settlers at Tubac before 1779 since there are reports that those settlers abandoned[28] Tubac during that year. In order to reestablish the presidio around 1800, Mexico began granting land for farm use to individuals with the provision that they would serve as soldiers when necessary. The state also apparently encouraged "squatters" by a policy of granting land to whoever farmed it. Thus, the land around Tubac was repopulated when a land rush occurred about the time of Mexican independence from Spain in 1820.

B. *Tumacácori*:

Originally built around 1700 as a Jesuit mission by Father Eusebio Francisco Kino for the Pima Indians, Tumacácori apparently developed a colony of settlers over the years. In 1751 when the Pima Indians revolted[29] they killed two priests and about 100 "settlers." The mission closed and the civilian settlers evacuated, but the mission was later moved from the east side to the west side of the Santa Cruz River. It is not known if the colonists returned when the mission was moved. On August 20, 1775 Juan Batista de Anza began leading about 300 settlers and priests north down the Santa Cruz River from Tumacácori through Tubac and Tucson to the Gila River and down the Gila to the Colorado River. This group traveled more that 1200 miles to found the city of San Francisco, California.

Tumacácori survived the loss of the 300 settlers since it once again suffered another devastating Apache attacked in 1801. It seems reasonable that new settlers would have come in during the land rush of 1820 along the Santa Cruz River. The US War with Mexico in 1845 to 1848 cut off supplies to Tumacácori from Mexico and California and, with the increased Apaches attacks in the region throughout the 1840s, by 1848

28   http://parentseyes.arizona.edu/tubac/app2.htm. Acc 6/26/2019
29   https://www.nps.gov/tuma/learn/historyculture/timeline.htm. Acc 6/26/2019

the last residents[30] left both Tumacácori and Tubac. At that time their land was not part of land that was ceded by Mexico to the US at the end of the war. The land south of the Gila River and east of California was not ceded to the US by Mexico until June 8, 1854 when the Gadsden Purchase was signed.

C. Tucson:

The Jesuit priest Father Eusebio Francisco Kino built the Mission San Xavier del Bac around the year 1700 about seven miles south of the present site of Tucson. The Irishman Hugo O'Conor, working for New Spain, built a presidio, San Agustín del Tucsón[31], in what is now downtown Tucson, near a site of a Pima Indian settlement in 1775. This presidio was moved from Tubac that summer due to a series of Apache raids in the region. [The Apaches were relative newcomers to the Santa Cruz valley, having been pushed westward from their home grounds in West Texas and eastern New Mexico by the Comanche Indians.] The year 1775 was when Juan Batista de Anza led the 300 colonists and priests from Tumacácori through Tucson to San Francisco, but there is no indication that there were any Spanish colonists in Tucson at the time.

Not counting the religious missionaries or the military men (and their wives and families) nor the camp followers, the first Spanish colonists in Tucson may well have been the "squatters" who moved in during 1820. This author is not aware of any "colonization grant" issued for any place in the Santa Cruz valley in the Spanish or Mexican period. Tucson, as well as almost all of the Santa Cruz Valley, became a part of the United States when the Gadsden Purchase was ratified in 1854. It was originally a part of Doña Ana County, New Mexico Territory until 1867 when it became the Capital of the new Arizona Territory.

---

30   http://www.nps.gov/tuma/learn/historyculture/timeline.htm. Acc 6/26/2019
31   https://en.wikipedia.org/wiki/Tucson,_Arizona. Acc 6/27/2019

D. Other Significant Settlements.

There were other Spanish settlements in the vicinity of Doña Ana County (see the previous chapter, page 38) in the early days. These existed primarily along the rivers and may not have ever been officially recognized as colonies. Among these is the settlement of Guebavi along the Rio Santa Cruz just north of the present international boundary between the Mexico and the USA. Guebavi was founded[32] in 1732 as the Catholic mission for the Indians but it probably had a Spanish population by about 1820. The same can be said for the mission at Xavier del Bac about 25 leagues (65 miles) north of Guebavi along the Rio Santa Cruz.

At about the same time as the presidio at Tubac was being established on the Rio Santa Cruz, another presidio was established along the Rio San Pedro about 50 miles north of the present international boundary. This was the Presidio Terrenate [33]and almost certainly would have had a Spanish settlement around it similar to the one at Tubac. An additional presidio was established along the Rio San Bernardino (called Cottonwood Creek in Arizona) just south of the international boundary about 20 miles west of the present New Mexico state line. This presidio was placed at the San Bernardino Ranch which extended far into both Mexico and the USA across the present international border.

---

32   H.F. Dobyns. Spanish Colonial Tucson, 1976. p 8.
33   H.F. Dobyns. Spanish Colonial Tucson, 1976. p 21.

Chapter 5

Doña Ana Bend Colony Grant

Several earlier settlements had existed in Spanish New Mexico in the land that would become the County of Doña Ana in New Mexico Territory of the United States. However, the first permanent settlement in the present State of New Mexico in the present Doña Ana County is the Village of Doña Ana near the north end of the county. This village was originally formed from part of the Doña Ana Bend Colony Grant under the authority of the State of Chihuahua. See the previous chapter for additional details. Even though general descriptions of the Grant had been made as early as 1839, it was not until Antonio Rey, the Prefect of El Paso del Norte, traveled to Doña Ana to set up the colony's government that an the official survey of the grant was conducted. On Jan 19, 1844 Antonio Rey started[1] at the head of Doña Ana Acequia and went south along the east bank of the river to the head of Brazito acequia; then went east to a point one league east of the foothills; then went north to a point east of Doña Ana Acequia and one league east of foothills; then went west to the head of Doña Ana Acequia, the starting point, to complete the survey.

This description of the survey may have been adequate at the time, but it leaves much to be desired for present use. For example, the course of the Rio Grande has changed several times since 1844 so it is no longer possible to know exactly where the west boundary of the grant (i.e. the east bank of the river in 1844) was located. Therefore, the location of the heads of the Doña Ana acequia and the Brazito acequia might now be in different places than they were in 1844. Also the east boundary of the grant would be difficult to locate precisely since it depends on Antonio Rey's interpretation of just where the foothills began at both the northern and southern ends of the grant. Another difficulty with Rey's description is his determination of "east" and "west." His "north" and "south" can be readily understood to be general directions since they follow the river or the line

1   J.J. Bowden. Spanish and Mexican Land Grants, 1971. p 70

from point to point along the eastern boundary. But Rey's cardinal directions require some scrutiny.

One of the last actions of Antonio Rey on January 25, 1844 was to specify a lot for the village's plaza. This was to be the northern half of a square of 100 varas (3291 inches or about 91.4 yards) on a side and laid out along the "cardinal directions." The southern half[2,3] of the lot was be used for the church. Rey also indicated that the streets of the village (and, presumably, the rest of the lots) were also laid out along the cardinal directions. However, inspection of the present locale of the Village of Doña Ana shows that all three features (church lot, streets and farms) are laid out along a grid that is rotated by about 30 degrees counter-clockwise from true north. This is an indication that Antonio Rey used the "rotated" grid as his "cardinal points" so that his "east" and "west" would be the 30 degrees off from the grid of modern maps. [This discrepancy could also be an indication that the village has moved and that the entire infrastructure was moved (and rotated) with it. However, I have found no other indication of such a full-scale move.]

The most likely cause of the rotated directions is that Rey was simply mistaken in his directions in 1844. While this may be interesting for determining original boundary positions, the present legal description of the land and lots is not determined by Antonio Rey's work for the State of Chihuahua, Mexico, but by the interpretation of his work by the US courts after the territory was obtained through the War with Mexico in 1846-1848.

The first sketch showing the relationship of the villages in the Mesilla Valley that has come to light is the one[4] made by Col. Joseph K. F. Mansfield in 1853 when he was inspecting Ft. Fillmore. The sketch shows the villages of Doña Ana, Las Cruces, Mesilla and Santo Tomás but does not show any of the land grants. This sketch indicates that the village of Doña Ana did have the skewed orientation layout whereas Mesilla and Las Cruces are shown with a normal cardinal direction orientation.

2   J.K. Proudfit. Surveyor-General's Office Report No. 85, April 4, 1874

3   Doña Ana Bend Colony Grant (web site). 1/26/1844, Acc 3/11/2018

4   W. S. Kiser. Turmoil on the Rio Grande, 2011. p 83.

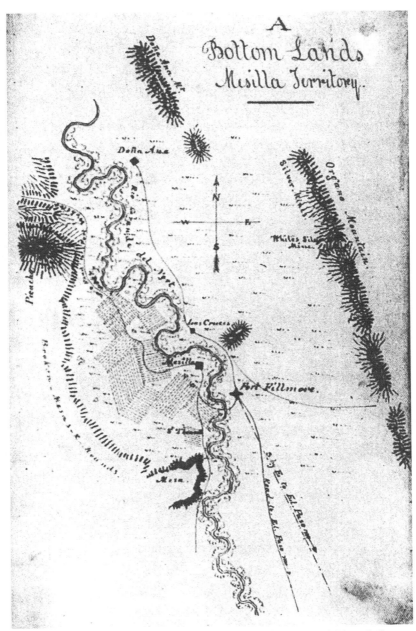

Mansfield's sketch of the Mesilla Valley done in 1853, while the village of Mesilla was still in Mexico, but Doña Ana, Las Cruces and Tortugas (which he did not show) were in the United States.

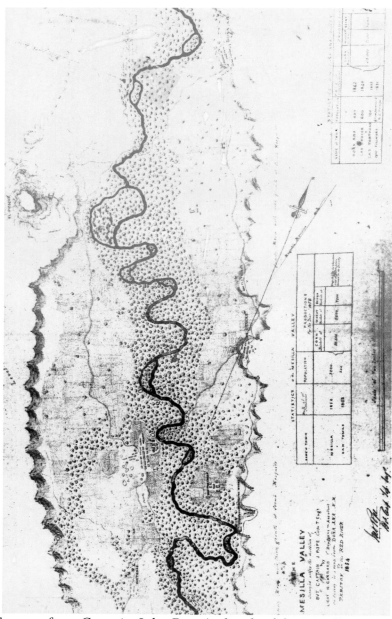

Excerpt from Captain John Pope's sketch of the Mesilla Valley showing Doña Ana, Las Cruces, Tortugas, Santo Tomás and La Mesilla along with both magnetic north and true (or grid) north executed in 1854. New Mexico State University Library, Archives and Special Collections.

The Mansfield sketch (also published in 1963 by Robert Frazer[5]) shows the course of the Rio Grande in detail as it existed in 1853 and it clearly shows a huge bend in the river for which the Doña Ana Bend Colony Grant may have been named.

A second sketch[6] of the Doña Ana region of the Mesilla Valley was done for Captain John Pope in 1854 at the start of his survey of a railroad route from the Mesilla Valley eastward to Preston, Texas. This sketch indicates true north and magnetic north and also gives a scale of miles as well as indicating the extent of the valley. It also shows the 30-degree misalignment of the Village of Doña Ana with respect to true north. This sketch was included in Mary Jane M. Garcia's NMSU Master's thesis "An Ethnohistory of Doña Ana" in 1986.

The two sketches by Mansfield (in 1853) and Pope (in 1854) give a fairly complete idea of the general nature of the valley and its population centers, but are little help in fixing the boundaries of the Doña Ana Bend Colony Grant (or any other another grant involving the region). Help with that problem would have to wait another 25 or 50 years while the people of the area dealt with some severe cultural and political problems and the uncertainty that resulted from those problems.

The Texas Question:

Before Doña Ana was founded in 1839 - 1843, the Republic of Texas had won its independence from Mexico in 1836 and had soon claimed all of Mexico's land east and north of the Rio Grande. Mexico never recognized those claims and continued to exercise political jurisdiction over those lands which included almost all of West Texas, about half of New Mexico and a significant part of Colorado and Wyoming. The threat of Texas' exercising its claim to the Mesilla Valley could have been one of the reasons Mexico was anxious to populate the region with it own people. Texas joined the United States in 1846 and the USA took up the cause of Texas' territorial claims and went

5   R.W. Frazer. Mansfield on the Condition of the Western Forts, 1853-54, 1963.
6   Rio Grande Historical Collection, Leland Giles Collection, NMSU. MS 0360.

to war with Mexico over that issue. The War with Mexico lasted until 1848 when Mexico ceded all of Texas' claims to the USA, but it was not until the Compromise of 1850 that Texas lost all its claim to the Mesilla Valley and all land north of the present state line between Texas and New Mexico.

The War between Mexico and the United States:

Texas joined the US is 1846 and very soon thereafter the US Army's General Stephen Watts Kearney invaded New Mexico to exercise Texas' claim to all lands east of the Rio Grande. (Lands west of the Rio Grande all the way to the Pacific Ocean were the undisputed territory of Mexico.) In August 1846 the US Army sent its Mormon Battalion[7] to New Mexico and well into the Mexican States of Chihuahua and Sonora and into Mexico's territory of California in a clear invasion of Mexico. By December 1846, Col. Alexander Doniphan had marched from Santa Fe, New Mexico southward through Doña Ana, (in the State of Chihuahua, Mexico) in the Mesilla Valley on his way to Chihuahua City. By the time the war ended in 1848 the US had captured Mexico City under Gen. Winfield Scott and had forced Mexico to cede the entire northern portion of its land (almost half of its total land) to the US, including Texas' original claims and as well as California and all of Arizona and New Mexico north of the Gila River and all lands north of there.

Apparently Article V of the Treaty of Guadalupe Hidalgo which was signed on February 2, 1848 and ended the war with Mexico, specified[8] the southern boundary between the US and Mexico west of the Rio Grande. This Article is understood to state that the boundary would start at El Paso del Norte and go west for three degrees of Longitude and then north to meet the Gila River and then follow the Gila to the Colorado River. However, the map which was referenced in the treaty was the infamous 1847 map produced by John Disturnell which contained many gross errors. The use of this map resulted in much misunderstanding and changing boundaries for the

---

7   G. Hackler. The March of the Mormon Battalion Through New Mexico, 2016.

8   W. S. Kiser. Turmoil on the Rio Grande, 2011. p 48.

next five years. Fortunately, the treaty called for a Boundary Commission to work out the actual boundary which would then become, retroactively, part of the Treaty of Guadalupe Hidalgo. But unfortunately, the Commission's (headed by John Russel Bartlett for the US and Pedro García-Conde for Mexico) work was repudiated by the US Congress and the resolution of the boundary would have to wait for the agreement known as the Gadsden Purchase in 1854. In the meantime, the Mesilla Valley west of the Rio Grande remained under the jurisdiction of the State of Chihuahua.

The Anglo Invasion:

Some of the US troops remained in the Mesilla Valley following the War with Mexico and started raising families. It also seems that some Texans had emigrated there and some of those tried to take over the land of the original settlers by claiming "Texas head rights" to the land. In addition, when gold was found in California in 1849, one of the main trails used to get to California was the Emigrant Trail which passed through the village of Doña Ana east to west. Some men quit the "gold rush" and settled in the Mesilla Valley.

The Mesilla Strip:

The name "Mesilla Strip" refers to the land lying between Latitude 32° 22' and Latitude 31° 52' North and approximately 3° of Longitude west of the Rio Grande. This is the strip of land between the boundary agreed by the Boundary Commission (but repudiated later by Congress) and (approximately) the boundary as it was originally thought to be established by the Treaty of Guadalupe Hidalgo (before the mistaken Disturnell map was adopted). A map[9] of this strip is shown in an accompanying figure on page 71 and is labeled "Mansfield's 1853 sketch of the Mesilla Strip" and includes the village of La Mesilla and nearly half of the entire Mesilla Valley. Although the Mesilla Strip did not include any of the Doña Ana Bend Colony Grant, the uncertainty of its international status probably had a profound effect on the people on both sides of the Rio Grande.

9   R.W. Frazer. Mansfield on the Condition of the Western Forts, 1853-54, 1963.

The Gadsden Purchase:

The issue of the location of the southern boundary between the US and Mexico was finally settled on June 29, 1854 when President Franklin Pierce signed the Gadsden Purchase agreement with Mexico. This treaty fixed the beginning of the boundary at the point where the Rio Grande meets the 31° 47' parallel of North Latitude and follows the present border line all the way to California and the Colorado River. It therefore included all of the Mesilla Strip as well as a sizable fraction of the Territory of New Mexico.

The Civil War:

After the Civil War erupted, the Confederate States of America took Ft. Fillmore on July 27, 1861 when Maj. Isaac Lynde ordered the US troops to march to Ft. Stanton. The US troops got only as far as San Augustine Springs at Organ before Lynde surrendered all 543 men[10] to Col. John Baylor of the Confederates. Baylor had occupied La Mesilla on the afternoon of July 25, 1861 and soon after Lynde's surrender declared all of the US Territory of New Mexico up to the 34° parallel of North Latitude to be the Confederate Territory of Arizona with Mesilla as its capital and with himself, Baylor, as its governor. This "Territory of Arizona" was the only "territory" held by the Confederates.

Six months later, in January 1862, Confederate Gen. Henry H. Sibley left Fort Bliss at El Paso, Texas apparently with the intent of capturing the gold fields around Cripple Creek, Colorado (which at the time were just a short distance from the New Mexico Territorial line). He fought his way up the Rio Grande valley, first defeating a superior force at Valverde (approximately 20 miles from the far northern boundary of the Confederate Territory of Arizona) on February 20 and 21, 1862 and then he occupied Albuquerque on March 2. He occupied Santa Fe on March 13 and then marched on to Glorieta Pass where he was defeated by Union forces on March 28, 1862. After the defeat at Glorieta Pass (or "Valley's Ranch" or Pigeon's Ranch

---

10   R. Wadsworth. Forgotten Fortress, 2002. p 330.

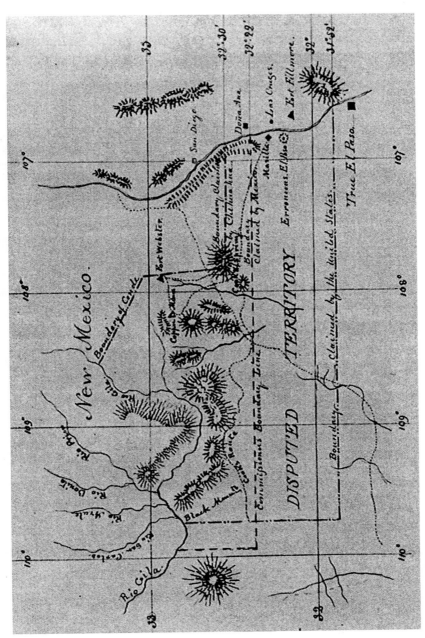

Mansfield's 1853 sketch of the Mesilla Strip disputed territory showing the difference between the boundaries tentatively accepted by the United States and Mexico after the Boundary Commission's work but before the Gadsden Purchase.

or Valle's Ranch) the Confederates returned to Ft. Fillmore and then left New Mexico. The Territory of Arizona reverted back to the US Territory of New Mexico.

The US Court's Decision on the Doña Ana Bend Colony Grant

The US gained control of the area that would become the Southwest USA in 1848 and, as part of the Treaty of Guadalupe Hidalgo, agreed that anyone who had legally held land under Mexico's jurisdiction would continue to hold it under the United States jurisdiction. Following the Gold Rush to California in 1849, California became a state in 1850 and the US found it necessary to settle the Spanish and Mexican land claims so that development of the state could proceed. In 1851 Congress passed legislation to address that problem, but the legislation applied only to California. The laws applied to California proved inadequate and prone to corruption. Congress then established the Office of the Surveyor General of New Mexico in 1854 in an effort to deal with the rest of the land acquired from Mexico. The implementation of those efforts were political in nature and also proved inadequate. It was not until March 3, 1891 that Congress established the "Court of Private Land Claims" to deal with the problem from a legal point of view. This Court was charged with sorting out the land claims in what were then the Territories of New Mexico, Arizona and Utah and the States of Colorado, Nevada and Wyoming, but did not include the state of California[11].

When Antonio Rey "surveyed" the Doña Ana Bend Colony Grant in 1844 his description remained the only legal description of the colony for almost the next 60 years. Unfortunately, his survey was referenced to physical features of the landscape which may have changed or have been forgotten over that period of time. Whatever the reasons may have been, the US did not make a legal decision about the ownership of the Doña Ana Bend colony or the ownership of individual parcels of land within the colony until 1901. One of the problems was the

11   https://en.wikipedia.org/wiki/United_States_Court_of_Private_Land_ Claims. Acc 7/30/2019

Townships and Ranges

Townships are square areas of six miles to a side. Each township is numbered according to it position with respect to a principal Meridian and a principal Baseline. The first row of townships north of the Baseline is designated T.1N and the first row south of the Baseline is designated T.1S. Likewise the first row east of the Meridian is designated R.1E while the first one west of the Meridian is designated R.1W. The township which is third north of the Baseline and fifth west of the Meridian would be designated by the coordinates T.3N, R.5W. Each township is divided into 36 sections which are numbered beginning in the Northeast corner of the township and proceeding to 6 toward the northwest corner; section 7 is just below (south) of section 6 and the sections east of 7 continue to section 12 (south of section 1): section 13 is just south of 12 and the numbers continue that pattern to section 36 in the southeast corner of the township.

lack of a suitable description of the colony's grant that could be referenced to longitude and latitude. The fundamental problem with that was solved in 1855 when the US surveyor John W. Garretson established[12] the New Mexico Meridian at 106° 53' 40" West Longitude and the New Mexico Baseline at 34° 15' 25" North Latitude. This Meridian and Baseline form the basis for the division and description of land into Townships and Ranges in the US. See the sidebar.

The first survey of the Doña Ana Bend Colony Grant by a deputy of the Surveyor General of New Mexico was done by Deputy Surveyor Clayton G. Coleman under Contract 313 dated June 15, 1897. This survey was done in support of a final decree by the Court of Private Land Claims issued on April 1, 1897 confirming[13]

> *unto Jose Maria Costales and certain other citizens, among whom are named the petitioners, Numa*

12   https://en.wikipedia.org/wiki/New Mexico meridian. Acc 7/29/2019
13   J.K. Proudfit. Surveyor General Report No. 85. Microfilm Reel 21.

Reymond, John D. Barncastle, Joseph Barncastle and
Manuel Banegas, and all persons placed in possession
of said property and such other persons as were bona-
fide residents upon the same at the date of said treaty (of
Guadalupe Hidalgo), and their heirs and successors in
the interest, the lands embraced in the "Doña Ana Bend
Colony" Grant, or claim, known on the docket of said
Court as No. 24, and situate in Ts. 22 S., Rs.1 and 2 E.,
Ts. 23 S, Rs. 1 and 2 E and T. 24 S., R. 2 E., Doña Ana
County, New Mexico.

However, after objections to the survey by U. S. Attorney
Matthew G. Reynolds, the survey was found to be "too faulty and
erroneous" by Thomas M. Hurlburt, the Examiner of Surveys
for the Surveyor General's office. It was subsequently rejected
on May 23, 1899.

The Surveyor General, Quinby Vance, next issued a
contract for a re-survey of the Doña Ana Bend Colony Grant
via Contract 352 on December 14, 1900 to Deputy Surveyor Jay
Turley. Turley completed his field survey from February 19,
1901 to March 8, 1901 and filed his report with the Surveyor
General on June 14, 1901. Both Turley and Coleman had
access to interviews and testimony taken from three people
on December 29, 1873 who had knowledge of the colony's
boundaries in 1844[14].

YRINEO CASTALES.

Irineo Castales, being first duly sworn, testifies as
follows: I live in Doña Ana, County of Doña Ana, and
Territory of New Mexico; I am forty-five years of age; I
know where the Doña Ana grant, ... is situated. It includes
within its limits the towns of Doña And, Las Cruces, and
Tortugas. The lands granted consist of the lands of the
Doña Ana Bend, (El Ancon de Doña Ana). Said Bend
extends from the head of the Doña Ana Acequia, above
said town, down Rio Grande River on its eastern bank, to
place on said river known as the Brazitos, where was the

---

14   J.K. Proudfit. Surveyor-General's Office Report No. 85, April 4, 1874

head of a ditch belonging to Juan Antonio Garcia, and where his grant commenced and extended south. Since the Doña Ana grant was made, the Rio Grande River in some places has changed. Where it has changed, I refer to the old river-bed, now known as such ... The said Rio Grande River was the western boundary at the time the said grant was made. The said grant of Doña Ana also included the foot-hills, on the east of the valley lands, described for pasturing purposes. My father José María Castales was one of the principal colonists of said Doña Ana colony. I know the boundaries of said grant, because I have been with parties when the boundaries were established, and the said boundaries have been recognized by every one, as such, ever since. My father took an active part in the colony, and I have my knowledge of the facts I have stated by being with him when he was engaged in measuring lands on the grant, and acting for the interests of the colony.

Sworn to and subscribed before me this 29th day of December, 1873. Witness my hand and the seal of court, the day and year last named. [SEAL] DANIEL FRIETZE. Probate Clerk of Doña Ana County, New Mexico.

FRANCISCO RODRIGUEZ.

FRANCISCO RODRIGUEZ being first duly sworn, deposes and says: I live in the town of Doña Ana, County of Doña Ana, Territory of New Mexico. My age is forty-nine years. I know the place known as the grant of Doña Ana. ... I went to said Doña Ana grant with the colony, when quite young, and have been there ever since. The grant afore-said was made to the land embraced in the Bend of the Rio Grande, known as the Bend of Doña Ana. Said Bend extends from the head of the acequia of Doña Ana at the north of said grant and Bend of Doña Ana, to the Brazito, at the south of said Bend and grant, a distance of about twelve miles north and south, up and down said river. The Brazitos is a point on the Rio

Grande del Norte at the northern limit of the grant now known as the Stevenson grant, formerly of Juan Antonio Garcia, and where the head of the acequia or ditch of said Garcia took the water from the said river Rio Grande to water lands of his said grant, that is the said Rio Grande formerly run there, but it is now changed. The Rio Grande River aforesaid, between the head of the Doña Ana acequia; aforesaid, and the Brazitos aforesaid, as it formerly run, that is the channel known as the old river, is the boundary of said grant of Doña Ana on the west. The eastern boundary of said grant is a line commencing one league east of the head of the said acequia of Doña Ana, and thence running to a point one league east of the Brazitos aforesaid, from north to south. This line embraces foot-hills which were granted to the colony for purposes of pasturage. ... The said grantees and their heirs have been always recognized by the authorities of the government of Mexico, and every one, as the legal owners and holders of the said lands. There are over three thousand five hundred persons now occupying and holding said lands by virtue of the grant of Doña Ana. Said grant was made by the authority of the government of the republic of Mexico. Said lands of said grant are non-mineral; they are agricultural and pastoral.

Sworn to and subscribed before me this 29th day of December, 1873. Witness my hand and the seal of court, the day and year last named. [SEAL] DANIEL FRIETZE, Probate Clerk of Doña Ana County, New Mexico.

GUADALUPE MIRANDA.

GUADALUPE MIRANDA, being first duly sworn, testifies as follows: I live in El Paso, Mexico, and I am sixty-three years of age. I know the grant called Doña Ana, or the Bend of Doña Ana. ... It is situated on the east bank of the Rio Bravo del Norte, known as the Rio Grande River, from ten to fifteen leagues north of the town of El Paso, Mexico, and within the present limits of the county of Doña Ana in the Territory of New Mexico. It includes the present towns of Doña Ana, Las Cruces, and Tortugas, ... The said grant embraces the lands included in and known heretofore as the Bend (Ancon) of Doña Ana. It extends from the mouth of the present acequias of Doña Ana, Las Cruces, and Mesilla, where the water enters said acequias from said Rio Grande to the barancas (high banks) at the head of the acequia of the Brazitos, (a branch of the river.) The place Brazitos is now known as the Stevenson grant, which is the southern limit of the bend of Doña Ana grant. The head of the acequias of Doña Ana, Las Cruces, and Mesilla, is the northern limit of said grant. At this last-named point the Rio Grande makes a bend leaving the foothills on the eastern bank of said river, and bearing southwestwardly and nearing the foot-hills on the western bank until said river passes the present town of Picacho, and thence said river bears toward the east and southeast until it reaches the "barancas del Brazito" before mentioned, which place was formerly the head of the acequia of don Juan Antonio Garcia, whose grant, now known as the Stephenson grant, commenced at this point, and thence extended south. All the land lying between the said river Rio Grande del Norte and the foot-hills on the east bank of said river, between the head of said acequias of Doña Ana, Las Cruces, and Mesilla, and the barancas del Brazito, are included in the grant of lands from the government of Mexico to the colony of Doña Ana. The eastern limits of said grant of Doña Ana are one league to the east of a line drawn along the foot-hills bordering on the east of said Bend of Doña Ana, running from north in a southerly direction, from a point opposite and east of the said northern limit of said grant, to a like point opposite and east of the southern limit as before stated, (one league.) This league of land bordering on the east of said Bend of Doña Ana, (one league deep,) was for use of colony for grazing purposes, and the lands bordering on the said river, bottom lands, were for agricultural purposes. The first petition by colonists to settle the Bend of Doña Ana, above described, was made to the government of Mexico in the year 1839. The colony was settled under great difficulties, and existed for a time under the most discouraging circumstances--chief difficulty being on account of savages or hostile Indians. At one time it seemed that the colony of Doña Ana would fail, but owing to the liberal grant of the republic of Mexico to the Bend of Doña Ana, a belt of land along the eastern bank of said river, a distance of about twelve miles, the colonists who had abandoned the place again returned with others, and have continued in possession of said grant ever since. I know the limits of said grant, because I, in company with the prefect, Antonio Rey, prefect of El Paso, in the State of Chihuahua, and Don Pablo Melendrez, measured off lands to the colonists. The colonists petitioned the government of Mexico for the tract of land known as the Bend of Doña Ana. Their petition was granted said colonists of Doña Ana, and the lands embraced in the limits above described measured off to them, all in accordance with law. I have reference to the course of the river Rio Grande at the time said grant was made. At the mouth of the acequias, at north limits of said grant, the river is the same but below it has changed, and the old river bed is the boundary of said grant on the west. In relation to said grant of Doña Ana, in the year 1846 I was prefect of El Paso, and by virtue of authority I had as such officer from the government of Mexico, I wrote the following to the justice of the peace at Doña Ana:

Sr. justice of peace of Doña Ana: "This prefecture being so much occupied by the incursions of the savages, and the personal services of myself being required in this town as of vital importance, I am not permitted to come to your town in person to the distribution of lands to your citizens, for which reason I send herewith to you the 'expediente' in the matter, in order that you may make the distribution of the lands and titles to them to the residents as well as those who shall come upon said colony within the time prescribed by the regulation, concluding that you will not make any distribution until you obtain permission, if it should be necessary, of the supreme government. "El Paso, January 22, 1846.

This letter had reference more particularly to the giving of title to the several colonists upon said grant. My acts, and those of the justice of the peace, were duly approved by the government of Mexico, the grantees of said grant of Doña Ana entered into possession of the lands before described, and they and their heirs have continually been in possession of the same, and have been recognized as the legal owners and holders of said grant of lands by every one since said grant was made till now. I know much about said grant, because I was an officer of the general government, acting as its agent (the government of Mexico) touching said grant, and it was deemed very important by the said government of Mexico to establish this said colony. I have examined the documents here, (document hereto annexes,) certified as copies of papers pertaining to the said Doña Ana grant, in the archives of secretary's office, State of Chihuahua, by Juan B. Escudero, secretary. Said copies are correct as far as I know. Many of the originals I have seen. The acts of the justices in making measurements in particular to individual colonists on said grant do not appear in them. They ought to be with the archives of the grantees. The two justices who knew much about the matter are dead--Don Pablo Malendrez and José Ma. Castales. The former issued the titles. The land measured off included what I have before stated. There are now upon said grant holding under it over three thousand five hundred inhabitants. The lands embraced in the limits of said

Doña And grant are non-mineral. I have no interest whatever in said grant of Doña Ana.

Sworn to and subscribed before me, this 29th day of December. A. D. 1873. Witness my hand and the seal of court, the day and year last named. [SEAL] DANIEL FRIETZE, Probate Clerk of Doña Ana County, New Mexico.

Primarily on the basis on these testimonies (particularly that of Guadalupe Miranda) James K. Proudfit, the Surveyor General at the time, recommended on March 31, 1874 that Congress recognize the validity of the Doña Ana Bend Colony Grant. But that did not happen until April 1, 1897 and it wasn't until after Jay Turley's survey in 1901 that it was approved by the Survey Examiner, Thomas W. Hurlburt, and recommended by the Surveyor General, Quinby Vance, on November 30, 1901 that it finally became official in 1904. Jay Turley's survey of the Doña Ana Bend Colony Grant was almost identical to that of Clayton G. Coleman and showed that the grant consisted of 35,399.017 acres. Title to the grant lands became unquestionable when the US government issued a patent dated February 8, 1907 (about three years after the Court of Private Land Claims ceased to exist),

> *subject to the reservation of gold, silver, and quicksilver mines and minerals, to its title in the following described lands in Doña Ana County, New Mexico, to the Doña Ana Bend Colony, its successors and assigns, to wit[15]:*
> *Commencing at a point on the east bank of the Rio Grande River, where the original settlers of said Grant took from the river the water for the Doña Ana acequia, being the same point at which the mouths of the Las Cruces and Mesilla acequias were afterwards located; it being the same point fixed by the Government of the U. S. Government survey as the northwest corner of said grant; then following the east bank of the Rio Grande, as that river ran in the year 1844, in a southerly direction*

15 http://dev.newmexicohistory.org/filedetails.php?fileID=24678#_edn-ref22. Acc 2/2/2019.

about 13 miles to a point on the east bank of said Rio Grande at a place called high banks, said point being the head or mouth of an acequia known as the acequia of the Bracito Grant (said Grant sometimes called the Hugh Stephenson Grant) and also being the southwest corner of the said Doña Ana Bend Colony Grant as fixed by the United States Government Survey, including all the lands lying between the said Rio Grande and the foothills on the east banks of said river, which are between the old head of said acequia of Doña Ana, Las Cruces, and Mesilla, and the said high banks and head of said Bracito acequia, also a strip of land one league in width lying east of a line drawn along the foothills which lie to the east of said strip of land bordering on the river, which said last mentioned strip of land one league in width is granted to said colonists for pastoral purposes.

Fortunately, Jay Turley included a plat of his survey when he submitted it to the Surveyor General and it is presented in an accompanying diagram. This diagram was included in Spanish documentation from 1840-1844 that was translated to English in 1874 by John D. Bail. This plat[16] shows the Rio Grande as it presumably ran in 1844 (marked by double lines) and as it ran after 1865 (marked by a single dashed line). It also shows the locations of Doña Ana Village, Las Cruces and Tortugas in the Doña Ana Colony Grant and Picacho, Mesilla and Fort Fillmore outside of that Grant. Although the note at the top is highly smudged, it might say, in part, "South of (baseline) and East of the Meridian of New Mexico". The page prior to this plat in the microfilm record is a page explaining the marking on the plat:

1. A, B, C, D: Commons or pasture lands belonging to Doña Ana Bend Grant

The lands lying between the Rio Grande and the line A-D are agricultural

A Head of the Doña Ana acequia

B Head of the Brazito acequia

---

16 J.K. Proudfit. Surveyor General Report No. 85. Microfilm Reel 21. p 848.

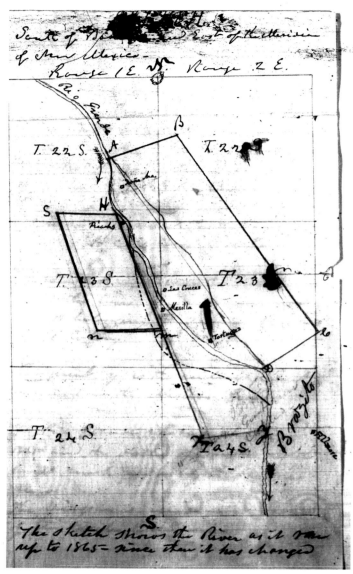

The plat showing what is believed to be Jay Turley's survey of the Doña Ana Bend Colony Grant filed in 1901. It has a notation at the bottom: "The sketch shows the River as it ran up to 1865. Since then it has changed". This diagram also shows the Doña Ana acequia and the Brazito acequia (points A and D) with a straight line joining the two. The east boundary of the Grant should be one league from this straight line.

2. H, S, n, m: Pasture lands belonging to the Civil Colony of Mesilla

The lands lying between the Rio Grande and the lines Y, X, H are farming lands belonging to Mesilla Grant - as Civil Colony

3. The point Y is the initial point named in the Mesilla Grant

4. The Rio Grande made a change in 1865 and the dotted line in the sketch would mark probably the course run.

5. The diagram is made in a scale of two miles to the inch.

The references to dates after 1844 imply that Bail or Turley or some unknown person probably modified the original diagram between 1874 and 1901 when Turley submitted his survey results. The fact that the original of this plat was made to a scale based on "inches" implies that whoever made the plat had copied the old Spanish document (or a modified copy of it) -- if, indeed, the original Spanish-language document had the (supposed) Antonio Rey diagram transmitted with it to John D. Bail when he translated the document.

Doña Ana

Chapter 6

Doña Ana Village

EARLY PEOPLE

Perhaps the story of the Village of Doña Ana should begin in 1682 when Gov. Antonio Otermín settled his colonists in the El Paso del Norte region after the Pueblo Revolt of 1680. Some of those same colonists went with Diego de Vargas in 1693 to re-colonize northern New Mexico, but the remainder stayed in the El Paso del Norte area and their descendents remain there today. In about 1828 the Rio Grande flooded and wiped out much of the farmland in the region of El Paso del Norte. This might have been the reason that in the early 1830s a group of about 20 men (perhaps including the ancestors of Roman Abeyta) came to the Doña Ana area to claim land as reported by Curry and Nichols in their book[1] based on the oral history and traditions of the region.

On September 18, 1839 a group of 116[2,3] citizens of El Paso del Norte (see Table 6.1), under the leadership of José María Costales, petitioned the State of Chihuahua[4] and its Governor José María Yrigoyen for a grant of land that would become known as the Doña Ana Bend Land Grant. The Departmental Assembly recommended granting the land, but nothing further happened during the term of Gov. Yrigoyen so a group resubmitted the petition to the new Governor, Francisco García Conde, on July 3, 1840. This new group consisted of 46 men of the first group and 70 new men who had not signed the first petition, so the second group also numbered 116 men. All of the men who signed the second petition are listed in Table

1 Curry and Nichols. Our Heritage, Our People, 1974. pp 10, 38.
2 James K. Proudfit. Surveyor-General's Office Report No. 85, April 4, 1874.
3 Doña Ana Bend Colony Grant (web site). 3/18/1839, Acc 3/11/2018
4 *When Mexico organized after winning its independence from Spain, it assigned the southern part of New Mexico from Carrizal to the North Latitude parallel of 32 degrees 35 minutes to the new State of Chihuahua. (See J.J. Bowden, page 2.)*

	Table 6.1 Original Authorized 116 Settlers of Doña Ana Bend Colony				
1	José María Costales	40	José Diego Canena	79	José Abalos
2	Lorenzo Provencio	41	Norberto Zamora	80	Juan Velarde
3	José Ma. Sierra	42	Benito Rodela	81	Gùereña the Suma
4	José Garcia	43	Teodocio Zamora	82	Guadalupe Valencia
5	José Antonio Ortega	44	Francisco Velarde	83	Remigo Saenz
6	José Ynes Corona	45	Francisco Lucero	84	José Antonio Provencio
7	Cristobal Provencio	46	Cosme Lucero	85	Evaristo Dias
8	Cano Lucero	47	Juan Agaton Herrera	86	Jesus Quilez
9	Rafael Rael	48	Francisco Sambrano	87	Julian Tellez
10	Miguel Garcia	49	Andres Maése	88	Francisco Tellez
11	Gregorio Davalos	50	Estevan Gonzalez	89	Apolinario Perea
12	José María Rodrigues	51	Ynocente Rivera	90	Jesus Cobos
13	Julio Arbayo	52	Esmergildo Cano	91	Eligio Tellez
14	Jesus Varela	53	Jesus Munoz	92	Martin Martinez
15	Felix Miranda	54	José Lucero	93	Ricardo Benavidez
16	Santos Abalos	55	Victoriano Sanches	94	Santos Trujillo
17	Brigido Provencio	56	Santos Jurado	95	Timoteo Montoya
18	Gregorio Herrera	57	Francisco Valverde	96	José María Lucero
19	José María Garcia	58	José Velarde	97	José Lucero
20	Narciso Varelo	59	José Bernal	98	Reyes Velarde
21	Nazario Herrera	60	Francisco Varela	99	José Antonio Cedillos
22	Manuel Padilla	61	Francisco Lucero	100	Antonio Salazar
23	José Delfin	62	José Blanco	101	Marciano Aldarete
24	Marieno Tellez	63	Mariano Trujillo	102	Juan Miguel Archuleta
25	Bautista Moya	64	José Montoya	103	Guillermo Varela
26	Francisco Lino	65	Cesario Acuña	104	Felipe Gonzalez
27	Felipe Herrera	66	Manuel Martinez	105	Timoteo Apodaca
28	Rafael Herrera	67	Rafael Lucero	106	Francisco Ortega
29	Francisco Rojai	68	Enriquez Llino	107	Ramon Alvilar
30	Victor Avalos	69	Tomas Carillo	108	Saturnino Campos
31	Bernabe Blanco	70	Eleuterio Perea	109	Ensebio Cadena
32	José Tomas Sanches	71	Marcelino Serna	110	Ynocente Herrera
33	Gregorio Martinez	72	Florencio Costales	111	Jesus Cordoba
34	Ramon Martinez	73	Luciana Melenudo	112	Rafael Herrera
35	Juan Jose Benavides	74	Francisco Garcia, blacksmith	113	Martin Lara
36	Wenceslas de la O.	75	Eustaquio Herrera	114	Cesario Duran
37	Benavé Montoya	76	Tomas Yrigoyen	115	Jose Morales
38	José Ma. Provencia	77	Pedro Garcia	116	Felipe Martinez
39	José Ma. Velarde	78	José Rivera		

The original 116 men who petitioned the Chihuahua State government on September 18, 1839 for a land grant to the Doña Ana Bend Colony.

6.2. Conde, after the approval of the Departmental Assembly, approved[5] the petition on July 8, 1840 and on August 5, 1840 ordered the establishment of the colony.

On October 19, 1840 another group of 32 Mexican citizens living in the nearby town of Senecú petitioned the State of Chihuahua for grants of land within the Indian settlement of Senecú. They were denied the petition on December 15, 1840

5   J.J. Bowden. Spanish and Mexican Land Grants, 1971. p 68

		Table 6.2 Doña Ana Bend Colonist as of 5/3/1840						
No. (6.2)	No. (6.1)	Name	No. (6.2)	No. (6.1)	Name	No. (6.2)	No. (6.1)	Name
1	1	José María Costales	40	94	Santos Trugillo	79	N/A	Santos Avalos
2	2	Lorenso Provencio	41	95	Timoteo Montoya	80	N/A	Andres Maese
3	3	José María Sierra	42	98	Reyes Velarde	81	N/A	Gabriel Gutierres
4	4	José Garcia	43	103	Guillermo Varela	82	N/A	Geronimo Lujan
5	6	José Ynes Corona	44	105	Timoteo Apodaca	83	N/A	Francisco Mondragon
6	7	Cristobal Provencio	45	112	Rafael Herrera	84	N/A	José María Cordova
7	8	Cano Lucero	46	116	Felipe Martinez	85	N/A	Romualdo Rojas
8	10	Miguel Garcia	47	N/A**	Ramon Dias de la Serne	86	N/A	Pablo Melendres
9	11	Gregorio Davalos	48	N/A	José Balverde	87	N/A	Casildo del Prado
10	13	Julio Arbayo	49	N/A	Yrinio Lujan	88	N/A	José Carbajal
11	14	Jesus Varela	50	N/A	Miguel Navarez	89	N/A	Cruz Martinez
12	17	Brigido Provencio	51	N/A	Juan Marquez	90	N/A	Francisco Horcasitas
13	19	José María Garcia	52	N/A	Severiano Varela	91	N/A	Vicente Manriques
14	21	Nazario Herrera	53	N/A	Ramon Cruz	92	N/A	Jesus Muñoz
15	22	Manuel Padilla	54	N/A	Francisco Rojas	93	N/A	Miguel Padilla
16	27	Felipe Herrera	55	N/A	Franco Lucero	94	N/A	José María Provencio
17	37	Bernabé Montoya	56	N/A	Florencio Benavides	95	N/A	Bantista Moya
18	39	José María Velarde	57	N/A	José Bianes	96	N/A	Balentin Gomez
19	41	Norberto Zamora	58	N/A	Manuel Lucero	97	N/A	Timoteo Barrio
20	47	Juan Agaton Herrera	59	N/A	Luciano Melenudo	98	N/A	Pedro Aredo
21	48	Francisco Sambrano	60	N/A	José Antonio Gallegos	99	N/A	Guadalupe Maese
22	54	José Lucero and	61	N/A	Antonio Apodaca	100	N/A	Antonio Padilla
23	59	José Bernal	62	N/A	Cesario Tellez	101	N/A	Pablo Madrid
24	61	Francisco Lucero*	63	N/A	Carmen Lucero	102	N/A	Bonifacio Armijo
25	63	Mariano Trujillo	64	N/A	Felipe Gonzales	103	N/A	José Avalos
26	64	José Montoya	65	N/A	Apolonio Rivera	104	N/A	Florentino Tellez
27	65	Cesario Acuña	66	N/A	Francisco Telles	105	N/A	Nepomuceno Hidalgo
28	66	Manuel Martinez	67	N/A	Dionicio Hidalgo	106	N/A	Esmerejildo Cano
29	67	Rafael Lucero	68	N/A	Narciso Varela	107	N/A	José Ma. Rodriguez
30	70	Eleuterio Perea	69	N/A	Victor Gomez	108	N/A	Eusebio Cadena
31	76	Tomas Yrigoyen	70	N/A	Francisco Provencio	109	N/A	José Ma. Morga
32	77	Pedro Garcia	71	N/A	Jesus Quiles	110	N/A	Jesus Duran
33	78	José Rivera	72	N/A	Juan Bautista	111	N/A	Ramon Padilla
34	83	José Remigio Saenz	73	N/A	Monico Benavides	112	N/A	Feliciano Ramirez
35	84	José Antonio Provencio	74	N/A	Gregorian Herrera	113	N/A	Juan Lucero
36	85	Evaristo Dias	75	N/A	Ponciano Velarde	114	N/A	José Diego Cadena
37	87	Julian Tellez	76	N/A	Pedro Gonzales	115	N/A	Mauricio Acosta
38	90	Jesus Cobos	77	N/A	Panfilo Tallez	116	N/A	Vicente Provencio
39	91	Eligio Tellez	78	N/A	José Antonio Madrid			
*	Table 6.1 lists two individuals named "Francisco Lucero" (no. 45 and no 61), but only one is listed in Table 6.2.							
**	N/A in this table implies that these individuals were not incolude in Table 6.1.							

When the Chihuahua government failed to act on the previous petition, another group of men from El Paso del Norte re-applied the land grant for the Doña Ana Bend region. This group also numbered 116 men, but only 46 of the original 116 were among those applicants on the second petition. It appears that 70 men had opted out of the venture in the eight months since the original petition. However, 70 new men were found to sign the new petition so that the number of men remained the same.

but were promised land grants[6,7] in the Doña Ana Bend Colony grant. See Table 6.3 for the names of these 32 men.

6   James K. Proudfit. Surveyor-General's Office Report No. 85, April 4, 1874.

7   Doña Ana Bend Colony Grant (web site). 10/19/1840, Acc 3/11/2018

Table 6.3 Senecú Thirty-two			
117	Pascual de la O.	133	Jose Blas Rivera
118	Candelario Gonzales	134	Teodoro Benavidez
119	Juan Anto. Garcia	135	Anastacio Cando
120	Saturnino Alvillan	136	Tomas Griego
121	Marcelo Orosco	137	José de los Angeles Curero
122	Calixtro Leyva	138	José Javela
123	Encamacion Romero	139	José Velarde
124	José Ma. Gonzalez	140	José Feliz Lopez
125	Pablo Alvillar	141	Gregorio Montoya
126	Juan Pablo Arce de Madrid	142	Antonio Jaramillo
127	Jose Vicente Lopez	143	Bautista Griego
128	Cristobal Orosco	144	Silvestre Pasos
129	Nicolas Pacheco	145	Eugenio Lopez
130	Gabriel Cordero	146	José Soto
131	José Blas Duran	147	Cosme Rios
132	Simon Guerra	148	Valentin Maese

The third group of men who were promised land in the new Doña Ana Bend Colony.

It appears that a total of 148 men with their wives and children were promised land in the Doña Ana Bend Colony. But before these men could take possession of the land, the hostile Apache raids increased which, then, forced them to request of the Prefect of El Paso del Norte an extension of the deadline by which they were to occupy[8] the grant from the winter of 1841/1842 (probably) until February 1, 1843. The Prefect granted them the extension on June 9, 1842 and on January 26, 1843 thirty-three of the colonists announced to the Prefect their readiness to proceed to the Doña Ana Bend. The Prefect appointed Bernabé Montoya to supervise the establishment of the Colony and authorized the colonists to occupy the land[9]. Among other things, Montoya was charged with dealing with other people wanting to join the colony[10]:

> *If, after arriving at the point Doña Ana, any citizens of this town or of any other town, whether of this or any other department of our republic, shall present themselves for*

8   Doña Ana Bend Colony Grant (web site). 6/9/1842, Acc 3/11/2018
9   J.J. Bowden. Spanish and Mexican Land Grants, 1971. p 68
10   Doña Ana Bend Colony Grant (web site). 2/2/1843, Acc 3/11/2018

the purpose of joining the new settlement, he will admit them, noting, in a roll he will keep, the names, day of their arrival, and lands they are assigned to.

El Paso, February 2, 1843[11].

It was obviously not the intent of the State of Chihuahua to grant land only to those signing the petition. Unfortunately, I have been unable to find a listing of these 33 men and their families who were the first occupants of the Doña Ana Bend Colony. We also do not know the date when the first settlers reached the colony but it was sometime between February 2, 1843 and April 15, 1843.

We do, however, have a list of 26 colonists[12] (see Table 6.4) who signed an appeal to the Governor of Chihuahua for help on April 15, 1843. These 26 men were almost certainly among the 33 who first arrived. If so, this would imply that not all the colonists signed the petition to the Governor. (This is also implied by the fact that Rodrigues, Zamora and Cordoba signed the original petition and the present petition of April 15, 1843 but did not show up on the petition of March 3, 1840.) It is interesting to note that none of the people signing the petition of April 15, 1843 were among those from Senecú. Also note that 11 of the names of Table 6.4 did not show up on any of the previous petitions. If there were actually 33 colonists at Doña Ana at the time, then seven men remain unknown. The petition that the 26 men sent to the Governor requested the following[13]:

1. That we be furnished with a detachment of troops for the safety of our persons and interests.

2. That we be furnished with a resupply of arms and ammunition.

3. That there be waived military service to which some of our companions are obligated.

4. That we be exempted from the taxes we suffer.

---

11   Doña Ana Bend Colony Grant (web site). 2/2/1843, Acc 3/11/2018

12   Doña Ana Bend Colony Grant (web site). 4/15/1843, Acc 3/11/2018

13   Doña Ana Bend Colony Grant (web site). 4/15/1843, Acc 3/11/2018

No. (6.4)	name	No. (6.1)	No. (6.2)	No. (6.3)	New Man
	**Table 6.4 Doña Ana Colonists as of April 15, 1843**				
1	José María Costales	1	1	N/P	
2	José María Sierra	3	3	N/P	
3	José Ynes Corona	6	5	N/P	
4	Gregorio Davalos	11	9	N/P	
5	José María Rodrigues	12		N/P	
6	Bernabé Montoya	37	17	N/P	
7	Teodocio Zamora	43		N/P	
8	José María Bernal	59	23	N/P	
9	Jesus Cordoba	111		N/P	
10	Ramon Dias de la Serna		47	N/P	
11	José Bianes		57	N/P	
12	José Antonio Gallego		60	N/P	
13	Geronimo Lujan		82	N/P	
14	José María Cordoba		84	N/P	
15	Pablo Melendres		86	N/P	
16	José María Lujan			N/P	Yes
17	José Tafoya			N/P	Yes
18	Julio Madrid			N/P	Yes
19	Miguel Nevarez			N/P	Yes
20	Pedro Aguirre			N/P	Yes
21	Eleuterio Perera			N/P	Yes
22	Felipe Madrid			N/P	Yes
23	Jesus Olivares			N/P	Yes
24	José María Valencia			N/P	Yes
25	Pedro Trujillo			N/P	Yes
26	Timoteo Mantoya			N/P	Yes
N/P	Implies not present at Doña Ana at the time				

A list of colonists who signed an appeal to the Governor of Chihuahua for help in setting up the Doña Ana Bend Colony. There might have been seven more men in the colony at the time.

> *5. That we be promptly furnished ten men from each district for the term of eight days so as in this way to finish the acequia, or that all who signed be compelled to repair thereto until its conclusion.*

6. That we be furnished the regulation by which we must govern ourselves in our new colony as was offered by the predecessor of your excellency.

7. That, should your high and increased engagements permit it, your excellency do us the favor to go and become acquainted with our lands, so that you may be persuaded of the advantages that would result to our department by colonizing them.

8. That if we cannot, owing to the shortness of the time, finish the acequia, we be permitted to go and cultivate this year the lands we have cleared, without prejudice to your ordering that the distribution of the lands be made, and that we take those which may suit us to put our property on.

On April 17, 1843, the Prefect of El Paso del Norte sent the Governor his evaluation of this petition, including the statement[14] in regard to item 5:

It is true all the petitioners have not assisted in the construction of the acequia, and only to the number of eighteen have done so.

On April 19, 1843 the Governor sent a detachment of seven soldiers with eleven muskets to defend the settlers against Apache raids. The Governor also exempted the colonists from military service and allowed them to cultivate, in common, the land they had already cleared without prejudicing their rights to individual land grants which were still to come. The Governor was unable to offer the colonists any relief in taxes or in constructing the *acequia madre* which they were able to finish (at least to the cleared land) during the month[15] of April 1843, anyway.

Sometime after April 19, 1843 there appears to have been a rather traumatic event at Doña Ana Bend, judging from the fact that the Governor requested an official report on the condition there on August 14, 1843. Joaquin Velarde of El Paso del Norte responded on October 30, 1843 saying there were only 14

14   Doña Ana Bend Colony Grant (web site). 4/17/1843, Acc 3/11/2018
15   J.J. Bowden. Spanish and Mexican Land Grants, 1971. p 69

residents[16] at that time and that they were the "first settlers," but I have found no record of their identities earlier than that given by Maude Elizabeth McFie in her history[17] of the Mesilla Valley written in 1903 and repeated in the 2019 calender[18] produce by the Doña Ana Village Historical Preservation Committee. The list of the colonists they give (without reference, other than tradition) is:

Pablo Melendres	José María Costales
Geronimo Lujan	Francisco Lucero
Juan José Benavidez	Francisco Rodriquez
Jesus Olivares	José María Bernal.
José María Perea	Saturnino Abillar
José Ines Garcia	Gabriel Davalos
Ramon de la Serna	1 other, name unknown

Velarde did not mention what happened to the others colonists except to say they were "restrained from doing so by a justified fear of suffering an aggression of the Apaches or Comanches, which they themselves could not resist." Lorenzo Provencio, a citizen of Doña Ana (perhaps the "1 other, name unknown"), requested[19] "of the commanding general a detachment of troops larger than the present one; for its protection." With this added protection, Doña Ana Bend Colony was expected to gain population and to be self-sustainable within "a couple of years."

I have found no record of this request for more troops being honored, but on January 9, 1844 another group of 55 Doña Ana colonists (see Table 6.5) signed a petition to Antonio Rey, the Prefect of the District of El Paso. This group was led by José María Costales and identified themselves as "new settlers of this colony" and requested "oxen and peons sufficient to work with." The group noted that "we have not completed the acequia to the point where it should be" but they thought it would be completed within five or six days. The main request was that the Prefect come to Doña Ana to distribute the land in time to

16   J.J. Bowden says the population was 14 by April 16, 1843, p 68.
17   M.E. McFie (Bloom). A History of the Mesilla Valley - 1903. p 19.
18   Doña Ana Historical 2019 Calendar.
19   Doña Ana Bend Colony Grant (web site). 10/30/1843, Acc 3/11/2018

Col. No.	Colonist Name	Table 6.1	Table 6.2	Table 6.3	Table 6.4
	Table 6.5 Santa Maria de Doña Ana, January 9, 1844.				
1	Agapito Vargas	*	*	*	*
2	Anastacio Minjares	*	*	*	*
3	Antonio Gallegos	*	60	*	12
4	Blas Provencio	*	*	*	*
5	Canuto	*	*	*	*
6	Casildo del Prado by Ramon Dias de la Serna	*	66	*	*
7	Cornelio Dias	*	*	*	*
8	Cristobal Provencio	7	30	*	*
9	Cruz Mauriquez	*	70	*	*
10	Dionicio Alvarado	*	*	*	*
11	Dionicioi Alvarado, for my son	*	*	*	*
12	Elenterio Perea	70	68	*	*
13	Esmerijildo Montoya	*	*	*	*
14	Felipe Madrid	*	*	*	*
15	Fernando Provencio	*	*	*	*
16	Francisco Rodriguez	*	*	*	*
17	Gabriel Avalos	*	*	*	*
18	Geronimo Lujan	*	82	*	13
19	Gregorio Brusuelas	*	*	*	*
20	Gregorio Davalos	11	9	*	4
21	Gregorio Montoya	*	*	141	*
22	Jesus Giles (Guiles)(Quilez)	86	41	*	*
23	Jesus Olivas by Cornelio Dias	*	*	*	*
24	Jesus Provencio	*		*	*
25	José Antonio Perea	*	*	*	*
26	José Antonio Provencio	84	79	*	*
27	José Apodaca	*	*	*	*
28	José Bianes	*	57 or 20	*	11
29	José Luis Madrid	*	*	*	*
30	José Ma. Barrera	*	*	*	*
31	José Ma. Castales	1	1	*	1
32	José Ma. Flores	*	*	*	*
33	José Ma. Perea	*	*	*	*
34	José Ma. Rodriquez	12	104	*	5
35	José Maria Bernal	59	23	*	8
36	José Perez	*	*	*	*
37	Juan José Benavides	35	*	*	*
38	Juan Lucero	*	113	*	*
39	Juan Maese	*	*	*	*
40	Julio Madrid	*	*	*	*
41	Lorenzo Baliseno	*	*	*	*
42	Luciano Red (Rael?)	*	*	*	*
43	Manuel Padilla	22	82	*	*
44	Manuel Provencio	*	*	*	*
45	Matilde Brusuelas	*	*	*	*
46	Merced Red (Rael)	*	*	*	*
47	Monica Benavides	*	46	*	*
48	Polinario Perea	*	*	*	*
49	Ramon dios de la Serna	*	47 pr 3	*	10
50	Reyes Perea	*	*	*	*
51	Teodoro Zamora	43		*	7
52	Timoteo Montaya	95	84	*	26
53	Vicente Garcia	*	*	*	*
54	Victor Minjares	*	*	*	*
55	Ysidoro Lujan	*	*	*	*
	* Not listed in the referenced Table				
	Numbers represent the colonist number in the referenced Table.				

Signers of the last petition to the Prefect, Antonio Rey, dated January 9, 1844. The Prefect of El Paso del Norte distributed the lands to the Doña Ana Bend Colony in January 19, 1844.

allow sufficient time for the planting of their wheat. Antonio Rey responded the he would start from El Paso del Norte on the 15th or 16th of January and on January 19, 1844 he started the measurements[20] of the individual lots which were to be assigned to each colonist. He finished the task and officially recorded the fact on January 25, 1844. The description of the colony's extent and the distribution of the land of the Doña Ana Bend Colony will be discussed in the next section of this chapter, labeled "Land."

On January 25, 1844, as part of the official land assignments in the new settlement of Doña Ana, Antonio Rey recorded the "residents and inhabitants" at the time. The following is taken from his records[21], maintaining his numbering but changing the format to make the listing more readable and correcting some of the spelling as it appears in the copy of the referenced record. This list is presented here simply because it is not generally readily available and it is one of the few records of the people in Doña Ana in the beginning. It may not be of interest to most readers but for genealogy researchers it might prove invaluable. The main line of the story of Doña Ana Village continues after the list.

1. José Maria Costales, 48 years, alternate justice, married to Nicolesa Ledesma, 48

      Children: 1. Marís Ysabel Costales, single, 19
                           2. Yrineo Costales, single,15
                           3. Langino Costales, single,12
                           4. Marís del Carmen Costales, single, 9.

2. Pablo Melendres, 47, principal justice, married to Guadalupe Horcasitas, 30

      Children: 1. Trinidad Melendres, single 11
                           2. Jesus Melendres, single,9
                           3. Pablo, Melendres, single,8
                           4. Josefa, Melendres, single, 6
                           5. Antonio, Melendres, single, 4
                           6. Liberato, Melendres, single, 2

---

20   Doña Ana Bend Colony Grant (web site). 1/19/1844, Acc 3/11/2018
21   Doña Ana Bend Colony Grant (web site). 1/25/1844, Acc 3/11/2018

3. Geronimo Lujan, 45, married to Guadalupe Valencia, ditto, 50.

Children:
1. José María Lujan, single, 21
2. Ysidoro Lujan, single, 18
3. Rumaldo, Lujan, single, 15
4. Juliana Lujan, single, 17
5. María de Jesus Lujan, single 5
6. Julianita Lujan, single, 9
7. Quirina Lujan, single, 14
6. Servulo Lujan, single, 2.

4. Eeuterio Perea, 52, married to Ramona Avalos, ditto, 40.

Children:
1. José Antonio Perea, single, 19
2. José María Perea, single, 17

5. Antonio Gallegos, 40, married to Leogarda Colmenero, 30.

Children:
1. Jesus María Gallegos, single, 16
2. José Ygnacio Gallegos, single, 14
3. Marcelino Gallegos, single, 9
4. José de la Luz Gallegos, single, 7
5. José Luis Gallegos, single, 5
6. José Pablo Gallegos, single, 4
7. Ma. del Refugio Gallegos, single, 12
8. Ma. Luisa Gallegos, single, 10
9. Ma. Luisa Gallegos, single, 2.

6. Bernabé Montoya, 60, widower.

Children:
1. Bautista Montoya, single, 30
2. Miguel Montoya, single, 27
3. Guillermo Montoya, single, 24

7. José Ma. Rodriguez, 35, married María Josefa Perea, 20.

Children:
1. Francisco Rodriguez, single, 18
2. José Angel Rodriguez, single, 10
3. Refugio Rodriguez, single, 8
4. Cipriano Rodriguez, single, 5

8. José Ynes Corono, 40, widower.

9. Jesus Olivares, 35, widower.

10. Ramon Serna, 25, single.

11. Casildo Prado, 20, single.

12. Cruz Manriquez, 16, single.

13. Julio Madrid, 56, married to Magdalena Alvillar, 25.

Children:
1. Andres Madrid, single, 17
2. Manuel Madrid, single, 9
3. Nicolas Madrid, single, 12
4. Felix Madrid, single, 6
5. José Madrid, single, 5
6. Florencio Madrid, single, 2

14. José Ma. Bernal, 31, married to Barbara Aguirre, 25.

15. Gregorio Davalos, 45, married to Guadalupe Trujillo, 39.

Children:
1. Luciano Davalos, single 19
2. Josefa Davalos, single 7
3. María Josefa Valencia Davalos, sing. 6

Also
1. Rafaela Trujillo, widow, 48

16. Juan José Benavides, 16, widower.

Children:
1. Mariano Benavides, single, 14
2. Ysabel Benavides, single, 10
3. Mauricio Benavides, single, 6
4. Lazaro Benavides, single, 5

17. Manuel Provencio, 28, married to María Josefa Aguilar, 22.

Children:
1. Feliciana Renteria Provencio, sing, 14

18. Blas Provencio, 30, marr. to María Manuela Martinez, 28.

Children:
1. Juan Provencio, single, 5
2. Catarino Provencio, single, 1
3. Polonio Varela Provencio, single, 19
4. Marcos Provencio, single, 15
5. Jesus Provencio, single, 11
6. Luis Provencio, single. 9

19. José Antonio Provencio, 30, single.

Children:
1. Jesus Provencio, single, 15
2. Felipe Provencio, single, 10.

20. Cristobal Provencio, 36, marr. to Nicolasa Benavidez, 28.

Children:
1. Juan Pablo Provencio, single, 8
2. Severiano Garcia Provencio, single, 9
3. Josefa Garcia Provencio, single, 4
4. Josefa Pablo Provencio, single, 3.

21. Gabriel Avalos, 27, married to Jacinta Blanco, 20.

22. Juan Lucero, 57, widower.

Children:
1. Jesus Lucero, single, 16.

23. Gregorio Montoya, 30, married to Josefa Vargas, 25.

Children: 1. Margarita Montoya, single, 8
                    2. Refugia Montoya, single, 2

Also   1. Esmereildo Montoya, single, 25

24. Luciano Rael, 25, married to Damiana Alvillar, 20.

Children: 1. María Eucarnacion Rael, single, 1.

25. Manuel Padilla, 30, married to Micaela Yrigoyen, 26.

Children: 1. Josefa Padilla, single, 10
                    2. Augustin Padilla, single, 6
                    3. Santos Padilla, single, 4

26. Monico Benavides, 22, married to Quirina Monriquez, 16.

Children: 1. Agustin Benavides, single, 3
                    2. Lugino Avalos Benavides, single, 16

27. José Apodaca, 30, married to Josefa Zamora, 25.

Children: 1. Canuto Apodaca, single, 4
                    2. José Apodaca, single, 3
                    3. Canuto Apodaca, single, 2
                    4. Felix Apodaca, single, 1.

28. Apolonio Perea, 25, married, to Florencia Montoya, 16

29. José Provencio, 31, married to Francisca Martinez, 19.

Children: 1. Teodocio Provencio, single, 6.

30. Francisco Lucero, 36, married to Simona Hidalgo, 29.

Children: 1. Clara Lucero, single, 13.

31. José Ma. Barrio, 19, single.

32. Gregario Brueselas, 52, married to Alvina Carbajal, 35.

Children: 1. Matilde Bruesulas, single, 23
                    2. Crisanto Carbajal Bruesulas, sing, 10

33. Estanislao Bernal, 18, single.

34. Vicente Garcia, 25. Single.

,   Children   1. Jesus Garcia Garcia, single, 5.

35. Agaton Silva (or Selso), 26, married to Felipa Madrid, 23.

Children: 1. Gregoria Silva, single, 3.

36. Teodoro Zamora, 33, married to Juana Alvillar, 24.

Children: 1. Juan Lucero, single, 16.

37. José Ma. Flores, 24, single.

38. Jesus Guiles, 24, single.

Children: 1. Jesus Perea Guilei, single,7.

39. Fernando Provencio, 20, single;

      Also: 1. Navora Velarde, 30; widow.

40. José María Varela, 23, single

41. Guillermo Varela, 50, married to Tomasa Herrera 30.

      Children: 1. Lorenzo Varela, single, 20
                          2. Silvano Varela, single, 16
                          3. Carmen Varela, single, 12
                          4. Rosa Varela, single, 8.

42. Timoteo Montoya, 43, married to Juliana Zuaso, 38.

      Children: 1. Eulogia Montoya, single, 12.

43. José Rael, 26, married to Manuela Hidalgo, 20.

      Children: 1. José Ponciano Rael, single, 2
                          2. Francisco Rael, single, 1.

44. José Luis Madrid, 45, married to María Candeleria Sanches, 35.

      Children: 1. María de los Angeles Madrid, sing, 15
                          2. José Ysidoro Madrid, single, 13
                          3. Maria Nicolasa Madrid, single, 10
                          4. Maria Petra Madrid, single, 7
                          5. María Francisca Madrid, single, 4.

45. José Dolores Madrid, 46, married to Rafaela Moreno, 30.

      Children: 1. Bartolo Madrid, single, 22
                          2. Dolores Madrid, single, 18
                          3. Agapito Madrid, single, 15

46. José Reyes Perea, 35, single.

47. Guadalupe Miranda, 33, married to Francisca Rascon, 32.

      Children: 1. Pablo Miranda, single, 12
                          2. Carmen Miranda, single, 10
                          3. Octaviano Miranda, single, 9
                          4. Refugio Miranda, single, 15
                          5. Elena Miranda, single, 12
      Also: 1. Vicenta Ortega, widow, 30.

48. José Perea, 15, single.

49. Desidereo Armijo, 26, married to Catarina Montoya, 19.

50. Victor Minjares, 30, married to Josefa Herrera, 22.

      Children: 1. José Minjares, single, 8

2. Polonia Minjares, single, 6
3. Nestora Minjares, single, 3.

51. Jesus Cordoba, 35, married to Josefa Escontriés, 33.

Children: 1. Antonio Cordoba, single, 13
2. Dolores Cordoba, single, 12
3. Jesus Cordoba, single, 10
4. Felix Cordoba, single, 10
5. Crescencio Cordoba, single, 7
6. Braulio Cordoba, single, 1
7. Nepumuceno Cordoba, single, 3.

52. Antonio José Apodaca, 25, marr to Ramora Armendariz, 21.

Children: 1. Jesus Apodaca, single, 3
2. Cristobal Apodaca, single, 1.

53. Jesus Provencio, 25, married to Refugio Morales, 23.

Children: 1. Ventura Provencio, single, 3
2. Gumecindo Provencio, single, 1

54. Ramon Cordoba, 25, married to Altagracia Garcia, 24.

Children: 1. José Cordoba, single, 4
2. Juana Cordoba, single, 3

55. Casimiro Aguirre, 38, married to Petra Gonzales, 26.

Children: 1. Maria Lucia Aguirre, single, 12
2. Josefa Aguirre, single, 10
3. Jesus Aguirre, single, 8
4. Pedro Aguirre, single, 6

56. Juan Maese, 45, married to Trinidad Cordoba, 23.

Children: 1. Lorenza Maese, single, 21
2. Francisco Maese, single, 15
3. Josefa Maese, single, 11

57. Cornelio Dias, 36, married to Rosa Contreras, 33.

Children: 1. Miguel Dias, single, 14
2. Lorenza Dias, single, 12
3. Gregorio Dias, single, 10
4. Guadalupe Dias, single, 8
5. Francisca Dias, single, 6
6. Evangelista Dias, single, 4
7. Silvestre Dias, single, 2.

58. Dolores Perea (or Perez), 18, single.

Also 1. Guadalupe Perea, 38

59. Victoriano Sanchez, 26, marr. to María Petra Apodaca, 24.
Children: 1. Pablo Sanchez, single, 4.
60. Onofre Varela, 21, married to Quirina Apodaca, 18.
Children: 1. Aristeo Varela, single, 2.
61. Felipe Madrid, single, 21.
62. Rafael Provencio, single, 20.
63. Lorenzo Balizan, 30, married to Josefa Vianes, ditto, 43.
Children: 1. Dolares Balizan, single, 19
              2. José María Balizan, single, 17
              3. José Dario, single, 15
64. Marcos Benavides, 18, single.
65. Cosmé Zamora, 60, married to Marcelina del Villar, 30.
Children: 1. Ventura Zamora, single, 25
              2. Ma. Eusebia Salazar Zamora, sing, 15
66. Agapito Vargas, 28, married to Faustina Lopez, 20.
Children: 1. Teodosio Vargas, single, 2
              2. María Guarda Vargas, single, 1
67. Apolonio Varela, 18, single.

Antonio Rey summarized this list as showing 44 married men and their wives, 5 widowers, 58 single men [of whom 23 were listed as heads of households], 15 single women, 48 boys and 47 girls. According to his count, there were 107 men, 59 women, 48 boys and 47 girls present for the census. On the list of households, there were a total of 3 widows and 145 children in all the households (including perhaps siblings of the men and women) but they were summarized as belonging to "single women", "single men" or they were not included in the 94 "boys and girls." There are listed, then, a total of 261 "residents and inhabitants" at the Doña Ana Bend Colony on January 25, 1844. Antonio Rey then returned to El Paso del Norte and on March 17, 1844 he sent a message to the Governor of the State of Chihuahua which included[22,23] the following statements:

---
22   James K. Proudfit. Surveyor-General's Office Report No. 85, April 4, 1874.
23   Doña Ana Bend Colony Grant (web site). 3/17/1844, Acc 3/11/2018

I directed the justice to order that all the parties interested to whom lands had been distributed, present in due time to this prefecture the proper papers which should be filed for issuing to them their titles, but up to this time there are but six papers; and this is the reason why I do not yet forward them for the approbation of his excellency. Finally, I have plainly observed since going to Doña Ana that the generality of the petitioners were discouraged, and that they did not justify hopes of earnestness in their applications, either on account of their poverty, or because they are not animated to carry out their undertakings. I now see my ideas already corroborated by the notice which the justice of the peace of the place has forwarded me, in which appear 31 citizens who have renounced their right, together with the corresponding families, amounting to 111 persons of all sexes and ages. That place is thereby again reduced to a very small number of inhabitants.

So it can be seen that within two months of previously reported census of Doña Ana, 31 of the 67 households had vacated the colony taking with them 111 of the 261 residents. This would have left 36 households with 150 individuals residing in the colony. Once again, I have not been able to locate the identities of those people who left nor of those people remaining on March 17, 1844 in the Doña Ana Bend Colony.

LAND

The land upon which the Doña Ana Bend Colony was established had been a *paraje* since long before the Spanish started using the El Camino Real (see Chapter 2) and had been used as a campsite by the Spanish almost continuously for more than 100 years before the colony was formed. When Antonio Rey, the Prefect of El Paso del Norte, performed his official measurements on January 25, 1844 he did not use landmarks that can be located today. Even the "bend" in the river has long since disappeared since the river changed it course in 1865 and was channelized after 1916 when Elephant Butte dam was constructed. The jurisdiction of the land changed from Mexico to the US after the 1846 - 1848 war and the US courts did not finally decide on its legal ownership status until 1907.

On the same day, January 25, 1844, that he announced the census showing 261 residents, Antonio Rey sent a message[24,25] to the two *alcaldes* (or Justices of the Peace), Pablo Melendres and José María Costales in which he said he would distribute 69 lots of land (for agricultural purposes) to those residents. He said he had laid out 47 lots of dimensions 780 1/2 varas by 780 1/2 varas (about 10.8 acres each) for those men who were heads of families and an additional 22 lots of dimensions 780 1/2 varas by 390 1/4 varies (about 5.4) for those men who were single. He also said that the larger agricultural lots were to

> *commence on the north side from a short distance this side of a branchy cottonwood distant 790 varas* [about 2194 feet] *from where the houses now are in the space between them and the mouth of the acequia, and on the south they extend from the further side of Las Cruces, about thirty varas* [about 83 1/3 feet] *this side of the little cottonwood.*

[The reference to "Las Cruces" certainly did not mean the present city of Las Cruces which was still about five years away from being founded. It might have might have been a reference to the crosses marking the graves for which the town of Las Cruces was named. (See Chapter 4.) That would have put the south boundary of the "larger lots" about seven miles from their northern boundary. This agrees with the 18 spaces shown in the "Plan" for the agriculture lands given in an attached graphic on page 103.] The Prefect did not otherwise describe the location or layout of those lots nor did he mention where the half-sized lots would be located, but it can be safely assumed that all the farm lots would have been west (downhill) of the acequia. But he apparently did produce a plan of those lots which was included

---

24   James K. Proudfit. Surveyor-General's Office Report No. 85, April 4, 1874.

25   Doña Ana Bend Colony Grant (web site). 1/25/1844, Acc 3/11/2018

in Jay Turley's survey report[26] of 1901. This plan is presented in an accompanying diagram and indicates the numbers of the 69 farm lots that Antonio Rey designated. It also indicates the path of the "National Road" (as the El Camino Real de Tierra Adentro was called after Mexico won its independence from Spain) but it is unclear if this path represents the "wagon trail" which the people traveled or if it represents the "stock trail" which was probably closer to the river and which was used by the herds of animals.

Antonio Rey assigned the lots of farm land to specific individuals on January 24, 1844 and he gave a list of which

26   J.K Proudfit. Suveyor General Report No. 85. pg 991.

Antonio Rey's agriculture land plan for the Doña Ana Bend Colony in 1844 as reported by Deputy Surveyor Jay Turley in 1901.

Table 6.6 Doña Ana Colonists Receiving Lots on Jan 24, 1844				
List No.	1st Name	Last Name	Lot No.	On Census
1	José María	Castales	9	yes
2	Pablo	Melendres	12	yes
3	Geronimo	Lujan	15	yes
4	Antonio	Gallegos	18	yes
5	José María	Rodriguez	10	yes
6	Eleuterio	Perea	13	yes
7	Julio	Madrid	16	yes
8	Gregorio	Davalos	19	yes
9	Ramon	Serna	2	yes
10	Jesus	Olivares	1	yes
11	José María	Bernal	69	yes
12	Cruz	Perea	68	NO
13	Ynes	Garcia	64	NO
14	Casildo	Prado	65	yes
15	Bernabe	Montoya	21	yes
16	Jesus	Cordoba	22	NO
17	Lorenzo	Balisano	25	yes
18	Juan	Maese	34	yes
19	Juan José	Benavides	5	yes
20	Monico	Benavides	58	yes
21	Antonio José	Apodaca	45	yes
22	Ysidro	Armijo	23	NO
23	Cornelio	Dias	7	yes
24	Victor	Minjares	27	NO
25	Gregorio	Montaya	46	yes
26	Cosme	Zamora	43	yes
27	Teodocio	Zamora	54	yes
28	Gregorio	Brusuelas	55	yes
29	Agapito	Vargas	11	yes
30	Manuel	Padilla	50	yes
31	Luciano	Rael	39	yes
32	Francisco	Lucero	31	yes
33	Cristobal	Provencio	14	yes
34	Timoteo	Montaya	29	yes
35	Apolinario	Perea	20	yes
36	Agaton	Selso (Silva)	17	yes
37	Juan	Lucero	30	yes
38	Jesus	Provencio	8	yes
39	José	Apodaca	26	yes
40	José Luis	Madrid	3	yes
41	Guadalupe	Miranda	33	yes
42	Dolores	Madrid	41	yes
43	Esmerejildo	Montaya	61	NO
44	José María	Barrio	62	yes
45	Estanislao	Bernal	60	yes
46	Dolores	Perez	40	yes
47	José	Perez	40	yes
48	Fernando	Provencio	28	yes
49	José Reyes	Perea	63	yes
50	Vicente	Garcia	36	yes
51	Juan María	Flores	24	yes
52	Rafael	Provencio	56	yes
53	Longino	Avalos	59	NO
54	Florencio	Benavides	37	NO
55	Manuel	Provencio	49	yes
56	Blas	Provencio	38	yes
57	José Antonio	Provencio	52	yes
58	Gabriel	Avalos	35	yes
59	Guillermo	Varela	53	yes
60	José	Rael	42	yes
61	Ramon	Cordóba	51	yes
62	Casimiro	Aguirre	6	yes
63	Victoriano	Sanches	47	yes
64	Onofre	Varela	57	yes
65	Felipe	Madrid	32	yes
66	Marcos	Benavides	67	yes
67	Apolonio	Varela	66	yes
68	Jesus	Guiles	44	yes

The farm lot assignments to individual colonists of the Doña Ana Bend Colony made by Prefect Antonio Rey in 1844. Not all persons appearing on census appear here but eight additional individuals do.

colonists received the numbered lots. This list is presented in Table 6.6. It is interesting to note that the list contains 68 individuals, 8 of whom were not listed among the 67 listed in the census, given previously, whereas Rey apparently planned to assign lots to 69 individuals. According to this list, lots 4 and 48 were not assigned to colonists. At this point in time, it is not possible to determine the exact location of the various lots because Antonio Rey referenced his measures to existing houses and to trees which have long since disappeared. Perhaps the best clue lies in the present time-honored local tradition as to the ownership of the various parcels of land in the area.

Immediately after Antonio Rey distributed the agricultural land, he set about establishing the town of Doña Ana for the colonists. The only hint he gave pertaining to the location of the town is in this note to the Justices of the Peace:

> To form the settlement I have selected an elevation which, although it does not quite meet my wish, from its circumstances seems at present to be the place most suitable. It possesses a fair view, overlooks a large portion of the fields, and I promise myself that its inhabitants will always enjoy the best health.

After receiving a response from the alcaldes Melendres and Costales, Rey set the limits of jurisdiction for the colony:

> I designate as jurisdiction to this new settlement of Doña Ana, 2,500 varas [6944.4 feet] toward the north, and the same toward the south: 1,250 [3472.2 feet] toward the east, and an equal number toward the west, counting from the center of the main plaza assigned to said settlement.

One of the last things that the Prefect did on January 25, 1844 was to designate a lot for the church and a house for the priest.

> a square of 100 varas in length and 50 in width, upon which said edifices may be erected, which square is situated in the plaza on the side looking to the south, its boundaries being toward the cardinal points.

All of this was in conformance with Articles 4 and 5 of a letter[27] from José Rodrigo Garcia of the Geographical Bureau of the State of Chihuahua of July 30, 1840 which authorized the formation of the colony:

> ART. 4. For the better regularity of the town, the honorable prefect will take care to divide it off in squares of one hundred varas in length and fifty in breadth, with streets between of twelve and a half varas of width.

> ART. 5. Each one of the present petitioners will be favored with the half of a square, or a surface of fifty varas on a side, that he may locate his residence thereon --- taking care that these possessions are adjoining one to the other for the better security of the place. In the most central part of the latter there will be taken four squares; two that are adjoining lengthwise will form the plaza, and the other two will be appropriated for the town-house, church, and minister's residence, when there shall be any.

The village encompassed an area 5,000 varas by 2500 varas or about 12,500,000 square varas or about 12.5 *labors* of land. That is equivalent to 2213.75 acres or 3.46 square miles (or sections). The total area of the Doña Ana Bend Colony Grant was officially calculated to be 35,399.017 acres or 55.31 square miles (see the previous chapter) so that the village, as set up by Antonio Rey, took up about 6.25% of the grant's land mass area.

In one of references[28], there is a plan (or partial plan around the plaza) of the village of Doña Ana. It shows the plaza in the center of the plan, but only 136 town lots of 50 varas by 50 varas with streets of 12 vara width between them. Unfortunately, I have not yet been able to uncover who was assigned to which lot for building their house in the village. Thus the plan covers only about 75 acres of the 2213.75 acres covered in the jurisdiction of the *alcaldes*. This plan is presented below under the title "Plan of the Town of Doña Ana" and may be due to Antonio Rey and

27   J.K. Proudfit. Surveyor-General's Office Report No. 85, July 30, 1840
28   J.K. Proudfit. Surveyor-General's Office Report No. 85 . p 21-1063.

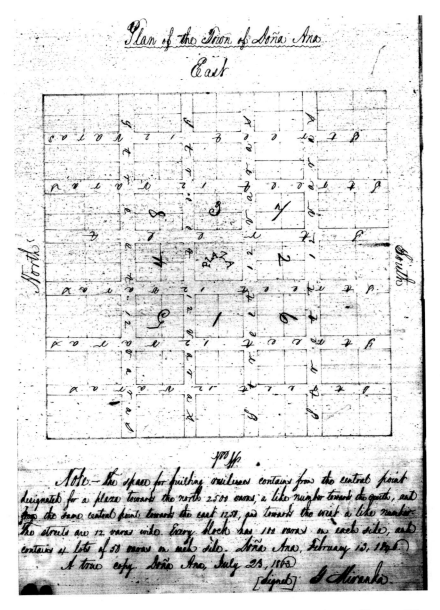

The town lot plan showing the layout of Doña Ana village. The
plaza is shown in the center, but it is unknown to whom the
individual lots were assigned.

was included in Jay Turley's survey notes in 1901. It is a copy and translation made by G(uadalupe) Miranda in July 23, 1863 of an original presumably produced on February 13, 1846.

When the Prefect of El Paso del Norte, Antonio Rey, authorized the colonists to occupy the Doña Ana Bend Colony Grant in 1843 he had appointed Barnabé Montoya to be his representative with instructions[29]:

> *If, after arriving at the point Doña Ana, any citizens of this town or of any other town, whether of this or any other department of our republic, shall present themselves for the purpose of joining the new settlement, he will admit them, noting, in a roll he will keep, the names, day of their arrival, and lands they are assigned to.*

Rey apparently anticipated that the entire Grant would eventually be claimed and he set up a mechanism to accomplish that. Montoya's authority presumably extended over the whole of the Grant and not just to the village of Doña Ana (which had not yet been established at that time). This, then, gave him authority to grant lands outside of the 3.46 sections designated for the village to later arrivals. The land surrounding the village of Doña Ana to the extent of 5,000 varas by 2500 varas (3.46 sections) would presumably come under the authority of the *alcaldes* to distribute to later arrivals. In addition to citizens of Mexico, who seem to have been coming and going throughout the early years of the colony up to 1848, these later arrivals would include US military forces starting in 1846, the California gold rush drop-outs of 1849, Confederate troops in 1861-62, railroad workers in about 1881 and many others including ranchers, farmers, outlaws, lawmen, churchmen, politicians and claim-jumpers.

The first known image of how the village may have appeared in the early days is an artist's rendition by an unknown artist presumably with Andrew B. Gray's (the chief surveyor[30] on the boundary commission) party in 1854. This piece of Gray's documentation[31] is shown in an accompanying figure

29   J.K. Proudfit. Surveyor-General's Office Report No. 85, Feb 2, 1843
30   W. S. Kiser. Turmoil on the Rio Grande, 2011. p 52.
31   NM St. University Library Archives and Special Collection. MS 0339.

TOWN AND VALLEY OF MESILLA
NEW-MEXICO.

Gray's 1854 sketch of the Village of Doña Ana depicting Isaac Garcia Drive (probably) going through it, with the Doña Ana Mountains in the background. This image is often mistaken for the village of La Mesilla primarily because of the name on the drawing. Courtesy or New Mexico State University Library, Archives and Special Collections, Image No. 03390024.

titled "Town and Valley of Mesilla." This sketch shows the view looking eastward along the Isaac Garcia Road (also known as 2nd Street) which is the same street of which Mary Jane Garcia[32] paraphrased her 91 year old uncle (in 1986) Pedro Madrid as saying:

> *The street that lies immediately south of the old historic church, Our Lady of Purification, is the same street that John Russell Bartlett described as main street on which were built good abode buildings for use by the military and for businesses (Bartlett, 1965 p. 212).*

This street was probably the path of the road to San Augustin Pass through the Organ Mountains (later called the Immigrant's Trail) to the east that led westward through Spring Canyon and on to California. This sketch has been published numerous times

---

32   M. J. Garcia. An Ethnohistory of Doña Ana, 1986. p 10.

The Gray Sketch of the Village of Doña Ana

The mountains in the background of this sketch are the Doña Ana mountains (with some artistic license taken by the artist) and are not the Organ Mountains which are east of Mesilla and which are shown in the bottom photograph.

Doña Ana Mountains at Doña Ana

Omitted in Gray's Sketch

Organ Mountains at Mesilla

Note the church bell tower midway on the left row of buildings. In 1854 the church in La Mesilla would have been on the right side of the sketch. Also, the Rio Grande would have run between the mountains and La Mesilla, but in the sketch the mesquite sand hills east of Doña Ana are shown. The conclusion is that the sketch represents Doña Ana in the "Valley of Mesilla" and does not represent village of La Mesilla. The street depicted in the sketch is probably either Isaac Garcia Drive or El Camino Real (Dusty Lane).

in the past, but the subject village has always been identified as La Mesilla and not as Doña Ana. See the sidebar on this page for information on its correct identification. Special thanks are due to Dan Aranda[33] for pointing out this possible early image of the Village of Doña Ana sketched only about 10 years after its founding.

33   Dan Aranda. Personal Communication, Nov. 2, 2018.

LIFE

When the first Doña Ana Bend Grant colonists came to Doña Ana in 1843 (or perhaps in 1842), they had to fight Apaches continually and they built their first settlement of Doña Ana in the form of circular enclosure, probably similar to the old Spanish military *real*. But this *"real"* was not made of tents as were the old Spanish military *reales*, but the individual houses were made of mud (*adobes*) or mud-covered, vertical sticks in typical *jacal* style construction. It would have had a circular enclosed inner courtyard to provide protection and the houses would have had openings only toward the inner courtyard or perhaps only on the roof[34]. The location of this circular settlement has been lost to memory, but there might be a hint in Antonio Rey's letter[35] to the *alcaldes* on January 24, 1844 in which he described the northern boundary of agricultural lots as

> *a short distance this side of a branchy cottonwood distant 790 varas* [about 2194 feet] *from where the houses now are in the space between them and the mouth of the acequia ...*

From this, we understand that: there was a "branchy" cottonwood tree standing in the space between the houses and the mouth of the acequia and it was about 790 varas from the houses. There might be another hint in Maude Elizabeth McFie's 1903 book where she talks about the location[36] of the townsite chosen in 1843 by Antonio Rey:

> *a place something a mile or two below the first location, and up above a high bluff where they were in command of the neighboring country.*

From these two hints, it can be understood that the first settlement (built primarily for defense against Apache attacks) was one or two miles north of the present village of Doña Ana which would place it also one or two miles below (south) the mouth of the acequia since the acequia began about three miles north of the present site of Doña Ana.

34   Curry and Nichols. Our Heritage, Our People, 1974. pg 8,
35   James K. Proudfit. Surveyor-Gen. Office Report No. 85, April 4, 874
36   M. E. McFie (Bloom). A History of the Mesilla Valley, 1999. p 17.

As an illustration of the harshness of life in that early settlement Mrs. Bloom (M. E. McFie) relates a story[37]:

> *It is said to be true of this long-ago town, that so crude was the manner of living that when General Mauricio Ugarte with his troops bound for the north [in 1842 in response to the invasion of Texans] arrived at the settlement, there were but four men to greet the company. These men were Pablo Melendrez, José M. Costales, Geronimo Lujan and José Bernal. The General inquired of the others and upon learning that they were hidden because they were completely destitute of clothing, he ordered them before him and generously fitted them out with his soldiers' clothing, gave them provisions, and a horse and a mule[38].*

In April of 1843, life started getting a bit better; the acequia was usable and the colonists planted crops and the Governor of Chihuahua sent a detachment of seven men and eleven muskets to protect the colony against Apache raids. Early the next year, the Prefect of El Paso del Norte distributed both farm land and town lots to the colonists and their families were able to join them shortly thereafter.

Significant Events by Year (to 1860):

1846:

1. On January 22, the Prefect of El Paso del Norte, Guadalupe Miranda, authorized Pablo Melendrez to issue title to the lands granted to each of the original colonists.

2. General Stephan Watts Kearny is given command of the new Army of the West and is ordered to take California and New Mexico.

---

37   M. E. McFie (Bloom). A History of the Mesilla Valley, 1999. p 17.
38   *I have not been able to corroborate this story with prior work. It is entirely possible that McFie was able to interview people who lived the experience. I do recall a similar story that said the other men went to the Doña Ana mountains to hide because they did not have "proper" clothing to greet a dignitary and were afraid to present themselves.*

3. US declares war with Mexico over Texas' claim to all land east of the Rio Grande.

4. Col. Alexander William Doniphan marched into Doña Ana with 856 "effective" men on December 22 on his way[39] to Chihuahua City.

5. James (Santiago) Kirker joined Doniphan on December 25 after Doniphan's Christmas-day victory at the Battle of Brazito[40] where several people from Doña Ana probably fought against him on the Mexican side.

1847:

1. On December 17 three soldiers[41] (Joseph Seraphin and two others) from Doña Ana were killed by Apaches near Point of Rocks north of San Diego Peak on the Camino Real.

1848:

1. "Another" wagon train[42] was robbed by the Indians near Doña Ana in early January.

2. The Treaty of Guadalupe Hidalgo ending the Mexican-American War was ratified[43] on July 4, 1848.

1849:

1. Even though some Dragoons were probably billeted in Doña Ana as early as 1847, it was not until August of 1849, that a military post[44] was officially established there when Company H of the 1st Dragoons under the command of Lt. Delos B. Sackett (acting for Major Enoch Steen) rented some adobe buildings near the plaza[45]. Sackett's Company B of the 3rd Infantry joined Steen's Dragoons on December 6, 1849. Company D, F and H of the 1st Dragoons and Company B of the 3rd Infantry

---

39   W. A. Keleher. Turmoil in New Mexico, 1952. p 121.
40   R. A. Smith. Borderlander, 1999. p 176.
41   R. P. Bieber. Marching with the Army of the West 1846-1848, 1936. p 349.
42   P.G. Ferguson. Marching with the Army of the West 1846-1848, 1936. p 351.
43   W. A. Keleher. Turmoil in New Mexico, 1952. p 36.
44   W. S. Kiser. Turmoil on the Rio Grande, 2011. p 99
45   W. S. Kiser. Dragoons in Apacheland, 2012. p 64.

Quarters for the Dragoons in Doña Ana

It is thought that the Dragoons were staying in Doña Ana as early as 1847. Originally they rented buildings "near the plaza[1]" for $170[2] per month (in 1848). In August 1849 a military post was formed and the post may have been moved to the "southeast fringes[3]" of the village. One of these places (if there were two) is probably described by Robert C. Garcia (one of the old timers in Doña Ana in 1974) when he said

> *One of the buildings in Doña Ana was built in the shape of a large "L". It was used by some of the calvary soldiers as a fort. Horses were kept inside the enclosure so they wouldn't get stolen. Some of the soldiers married the women here.*

as reported[4] in Curry and Nichols.

The post was likely kept in the same rented quarters[5] until 1851 when the rental fee went up to $362 per month and the soldiers were moved to Ft. Fillmore.

1 W. S. Kiser. Turmoil on the Rio Grande, 2011. p 99.
2 W. S. Kiser. Dragoons in Apacheland, 2012. pg 302.
3 W.S. Kiser. Dragoons in Apacheland, 2012. pg 64.
4 Curry and Nichols. Our Heritage, Our People, 1974. pg 10, p 49.
5 R. W. Frazer. New Mexico in 1850. 1968. pg 168

were posted here at various times until 1851 when the post was permanently decommissioned. See the sidebar titled "Quarters for the Dragoons in Doña Ana."

2. Probably before July, while Sackett was still in command of the post, he was asked (most likely by Pablo Melendres, the alcalde of Doña Ana) to survey sites for new towns, Las Cruces and Tortugas.

3. Company B of the 3rd Infantry is assigned[46] to the post at Doña Ana on December 6 and placed under the command of Major Steen.

<u>1850</u>:

1. In the Fall of 1850, the posting of Company C of the Regiment of Mounted Rifles brought the troop strength at Doña Ana to 97.

46 R. Frazer. New Mexico in 1850, a Military View, 1968. p166.

2. Texas vacates it claim to the Mesilla Valley in the Compromise of 1850 by agreeing to sell it to the United States.

1851:

1. The New Mexico Territorial Legislature created[47] the County of Doña Ana on July 10 with the village of Doña Ana as the County Seat.

2. Ft. Fillmore was established[48] on September 23 when Lt. Col. Dixon Stansbury Miles arrived there, but the site had already been occupied by some of Capt. Abraham Buford's Doña Ana troops in tents.

3. Later in 1851 Col. Edwin Vose Sumner deactivated[49] the post at the village of Doña Ana and transferred its troops to Ft. Fillmore. Apache raids against the town increased.

1852:

1. In December, the murderer of Dragoon Sgt. Graves was brought to the village of Doña Ana (then the County Seat of Doña Ana County) for trial, conviction and lynching.

1853:

1. In January Pablo Melendrez was still the *alcalde* of the Village of Doña Ana. At the end of the war with Mexico, the US authorities seem to have typically kept the same political structure that was developed under Mexican rule and left the same people in charge.

2. On February 3, 12 (or, perhaps only one) peaceful Apaches at Doña Ana were killed by Mexicans from Mesilla.

3. In the Fall of 1853 an Indian Agency[50] for the Apache was established at Doña Ana as a direct result of Maj. Steens efforts at Ft. Webster on the Mimbres River.

4. On November 6 Apache leader Cuentas Azules was murdered near Doña Ana by Don Pedro Borule for stealing a horse, but Azules was innocent.

---

47   W. S. Kiser. Turmoil on the Rio Grande, 2011. p 133
48   R. Wadsworth. Forgotten Fortress, 2002. p 35.
49   W. A. Keleher. Turmoil in New Mexico, 1952. p 56.
50   R. Wadsworth. Forgotten Fortress, 2002. p 97.

5. On December 30 the Gadsden Purchase agreement[51] was made after the Bartlett - Garcia Conde line had been repudiated.

1855:

1. The Gadsden Purchase treaty was ratified on June 30, setting the present boundary between Mexico and the US.

1858:

1. Several mules were stolen from Don Pedro DeGuerre near Doña Ana. The thieves were at first thought to be Apaches, but were later believed to be Mexicans from across the river near Mesilla.

2. On February 8, the Mesilla Guard came into the village of Doña Ana and killed several Mescalero Apaches[52] even though the townspeople tried to protect the Indians. The Mescalero's were permitted by the Indian Agent to enter to town.

The last battle between the Apaches and the people of Doña Ana was described by Pedro Madrid in an oral history gathered by Curry and Nichols for their book published in 1974[53]:

> *My father died when I was only thirteen, but I can remember when he told me about the last battle the men from our village had with the Indians. It was fought in the San Diego Mountains a few miles north. The Apaches were fierce and it was a very bloody battle. But they were driven away, Some of my relatives died.*

Pedro Madrid did not give a date for that San Diego fight, but it seems that the Apache attacks on the Village of Doña Ana decreased markedly when the Mesilla Valley population increased during the 1850s. The attacks essentially stopped altogether by the time the USA troops of the California Column arrived on the scene in the early 1860s. However, the Apache attacks continued in the sparsely populated portion of Doña Ana County until Cohise, Victorio and Geronimo were defeated.

---

51   M. E. McFie (Bloom). A History of the Mesilla Valley - 1903, p 10.
52   R. Wadsworth. Forgotten Fortress, 2002. p 227.
53   Curry and Nichols. Our Heritage, Our People, 1974. pg 10, p 31.

Chapter 7

Doña Ana County

With the end of the War with Mexico in 1848, the Treaty of Guadalupe Hidalgo spelled out a boundary between the two countries as an east-west line near El Paso del Norte, but, unfortunately, the treaty also adopted the 1847 map made by John Disturnell. Disturnell's map has many gross errors: it places the Rio Grande about 160 miles too far east at the position of the Pecos River and it places "El Paso" about 50 miles too far north near the actual position of Doña Ana. Fortunately, the treaty also called for the creation of a "Boundary Commission" which was to resolve any question and create the actual boundary position. Correcting Disturnell's misplacement of the river was relatively easy but the Boundary Commission's John Bartlett and Pedro García-Conde agreed to start the boundary line on the west side of the Rio Grande at latitude 32° 22' near Disturnell's (mistaken) placement of "El Paso" even though it was obviously wrong. That placement of the boundary did not include almost half of the Mesilla Valley. The Bartlett and García-Conde line was never accepted by the US and the area from El Paso del Norte to latitude 32° 22' known as the "Mesilla Strip" (see page 71) became a "disputed area" until the Gadsden Purchase was ratified in 1854.

Meanwhile, the Congress of the US accepted New Mexico into the US as a Territory via the Organic Act which was signed by President Milliard Fillmore on September 9, 1850. This Act provided for the formation of a Territorial Government which then created Doña Ana county as one of the original nine counties on January 9, 1852. All of the nine counties, with the exception of Doña Ana county, extended from the Texas state line on the east to the California state line on the west. [California had been admitted as a State in 1850.] However, since the jurisdiction of the region west of the Rio Grande and west of new Doña Ana county was still disputed between Mexico and the US, Doña Ana county extended from the Texas state line westward only to the Rio Grande.

ORIGINAL COUNTY BOUNDARIES

When Doña Ana county was created on January 9, 1852 the boundaries were described as:

> *The southern boundary, on the left bank of the Rio de Norte, is the boundary of the state of Texas, and on the right the dividing line between the Republic of Mexico; on the north, the boundary of the county of Socorro: and on the east and west, the boundaries of the Territory.*

The "boundary of the state of Texas" is 32° North Latitude, the "dividing line between the Republic of Mexico" was being disputed so would have been indeterminate until the Boundary Commission finished its work. The northern boundary of Doña Ana county was 33° 04' North Latitude[1], a line passing through the Ojo de los Muertos (or Muerto Springs) on the Camino Real de Tierra Adentro. (However, the southern boundary of Socorro County continued on that line until it hit the Gila River and then followed that river to its junction with the Colorado River at the California state line). The east boundary was the Texas state line[2] at 103° West Longitude (but this was changed in 1859[3] to 103° 03' 55" through a surveying error made by John H. Clark). The west boundary was a bit more complicated in that the western "boundaries of the Territory" were not yet determined by the Boundary Commission. Thanks to the mistakes on the Disturnell map, all of the region south of the southern boundary of Socorro County (at 34° 04') and west of the Rio Grande was included in the "disputed area" even though the very northern portion extending to the Gila River could have been claimed as part of Doña Ana county. As is usually accepted by the majority of historians, the Rio Grande was considered the effective western limit of Doña Ana County when it was first created.

Bartlett and García-Conde agreed that the southern boundary of the New Mexico Territory (and the United States) should lie along the 32° 22' parallel of North Latitude and extend

---

1   Scaled from Colton's 1855 Map of New Mexico.
2   W. F. Roeder. "New Mexico's Historic East Boundary" in Antepasados,
3   W. F. Roeder. "Perhaps the Most Incorrect of Any Land Line" in Antepasados, 1995.

three degrees of longitude to the west of the Rio Grande before heading north to meet the Gila River and then follow that river to its junction with the Colorado River. That agreement was accepted by the Mexican government but was repudiated by the US government, so it was never a legal boundary between the two countries. I have been unable to find any evidence that Doña Ana County extended into that area west of the Rio Grande until after the Gadsden Purchase.

After the Gadsden Purchase:

Even though the Boundary Commission's results were not accepted as the legal boundary between the USA and Mexico, it seems to have been "legal enough" to form the northern boundary of the Gadsden Purchase. (See Chapter 3.) When the Gadsden Purchase was completed its entire area was added to Doña Ana County by an Act[4] of the New Mexico Territorial Legislature on January 15, 1855 in accordance with the original definition of the county. The boundaries of the county now followed the southern Socorro County line from Texas to California on the north; the Texas State Line (at 103° West Longitude) on the east; the California State Line on the West; and, on the south, the Texas State Line at 32° North latitude from 103° West Longitude to the Rio Grande, then follows the Rio Grande (as it flowed on September 9, 1850) to 31° 20' North Latitude and then follows the Gadsden Purchase southern boundary to the Colorado River just below the present site of Yuma, AZ (see Chapter 3).

Doña Ana County maintained those boundaries from January 15, 1855 until February 1, 1860 when the Ninth Assembly of the New Mexico Territorial Legislature created the Arizona County from the western part of the county starting one mile[5] east of the Butterfield stage stop at Apache Pass. The stage stop was located at approximately 32° 09' 27.17" N and 109° 27' 17.19" W which would put the Arizona County Line at approximately 109° 26' 15.57" West Longitude[6]. Arizona County lasted only

---

4   G. B. Anderson. History of New Mexico, V 2, 1907. p 561.
5   Walker and Bufkin. Historical Atlas of Arizona, 1979. p 29.
6   G. Hackler. The Butterfield Trail Through New Mexico, 2nd ed, 2016. p 192

Arizona County, New Mexico Territory was split from Doña Ana County in early 1860 and existed for about two years. The boundary of Arizona County was about 30 miles west of the present Arizona State Line. Modern states are shown in green ink outlines for reference.

about two years before the Eleventh Assembly eliminated it by an Act of January 18, 1862 and its land reverted back to Doña Ana County. However, the Twelfth Assembly re-established Arizona County on January 28, 1863, just a month before it was abolished by the creation of the Arizona Territory[7] by the US Congress on February 24, 1863. The Arizona Territory was created from the New Mexico Territory by splitting it along a north-south line starting at the southwest corner of the Territory of Colorado and specified to be on the 32nd parallel of longitude west of the observatory at Washington, DC. This would put the split line[8] at 109° 03' 02.3" West Longitude (with respect to Greenwich).

7   J. H. Long. New Mexico: Individual County Chronologies, 2007. https://publications.newberry.org/ahcbp//documents/NM_Individual_ County_Chronologies.htm Acc 8/23/2019.
8   W. F. Roeder. "The Boundary of All These Kingdoms" in Antepasados, 1995.

Table 7.1 Doña Ana County Divided	
Year	Division
1852	Doña Ana County created to extend from Texas to California
1860	Arizona County formed from western part from about Apache Pass
1863	Doña Ana County limited by creation of Arizona Territory
1868	Grant County formed from western portion
1871	Socorro County extened south to 1 mile south of Caballo Mnts.
1878	Lincoln County takes over half of eastern portion
1884	Sierra County takes northwester part of county
1889	Eddy County formed from southeast portion of Lincoln County
1889	Chaves County form from northest portion of Lincoln County
1889	Otero County created from Lincoln Co and eastern Doña Ana Co
1901	Luna County created from eastern Grant Co and western Doña Ana Co
1917	Lea County created from eastern parts of Eddy Co and Chaves Co
1919	Hidalgo County created from southwestern Grant County.

Major divisions of Doña Ana County since its creation in 1852. The State Constitution has restricted changing of county boundaries (except for creating new counties) since 1912.

After Arizona Territory:

When Arizona Territory was created, Doña Ana County lost the land between the Territory line and the line separating Doña Ana County and the former Arizona County. The county then included all of the southern part of New Mexico Territory from 33° 04' (the southern boundary of Socorro County) to 32° (the State Line of Texas) east of the Rio Grande and the Gadsden Purchase line (west of the Rio Grande) and extended from 103° 03' 55" (the western State Line of Texas) to 109° 03' 02.3" (the new line separating New Mexico Territory and Arizona Territory). The boundaries of Doña Ana County remained at those locations until 1868 when Grant County was formed from the western part of the county by a north-south line drawn between Township Ranges[9] seven and eight and extending to the Arizona Territory line. Grant County was the thirteenth county in the new New Mexico Territory and was the first of many divisions of the new version of Doña Ana County. See Table 7.1 for more information. By the time Hidalgo County was created in 1919, the area that had been Doña Ana County in 1863 had been broken up into parts of nine[10] different counties.

9   Beck and Haase. Historical Atlas of New Mexico, 1969. p 43.
10   Beck and Haase. Historical Atlas of New Mexico, 1969. p 50.

EARLY COUNTY SERVANTS

When the War with Mexico ended in 1848, the area around the Village of Doña Ana was the only settled region in southern New Mexico Territory. It was governed by Pablo Melendres and José María Costales, the same men who had been the *alcaldes* before the War. The county was created in 1850 and Pablo Melendres appears to have continued his duties until elections were held in (presumably) 1852. A complete list of the sheriffs of Doña Ana County to the year 2000 was compiled[11] by Miguel F. Apodaca, a former sheriff (1941-1944), and presented to the county. A listing of the early sheriffs is given in Table 7.2 (through Apodaca's own term).

Perhaps the most complete list of other early county officials has been compiled by George B. Anderson[12] but he noted

11 https://nmagp.genealogyvillage.com/donaana/sheriffs_donaana.htm, acc 8/28/19
12 G. B. Anderson. History of New Mexico, V 2, 1907. pp 561-562.

Table 7.2 Early Sheriffs of Doña Ana County			
Year	Sheriff	Year	Sheriff
1852-54	John Jones	1887-88	Santiago P. Ascarate
1854	Thomas Chunton	1889-92	Mariano Barela
1854-55	Samuel G. Bean	1892-94	Martin Lohman
1855	Benjamin H. Read	1895-96	Guadalupe Ascarate
1855	Jesus Lucero	1896	Numa Edward Raymond
1856-69	Samuel G. Bean	1896-1900	Patrick F. Garrett
1859-61	Marcial Padilla	1901-05	José R. Lucero
1861-62	John A. Roberts	1905-08	Felipe Lucero
1863	Frederick Burkner	1909-12	José R. Lucero
1863-65	Apolonio Barela	1913-16	Felipe Lucero
1865	Reyes Escontreras	1917-20	José R. Lucero
1865-68	Mariano Barela	1921-22	Felipe Lucero
1869-71	Fabian Gonzales	1923-24	Donaciano Rodriquez
1871-78	Mariano Barela	1925-28	José R. Lucero
1879-80	Henry J. Cuniffe	1929-30	Felipe Lucero
1881	James W. Southwick	1931-34	Ricardo Triviz
1881-82	Thomas J. Bull	1935-36	José R. Lucero
1883-84	Guadalupe Ascarate	1937-40	José M. Viramontes
1885-86	Eugene Van Patton	1941-44	Miguel F. Apodaca

Early Sheriffs of Doña Ana County as listed by Miguel F. Apodaca, a former sheriff.

Table 7.3 Early Probate Judges of Doña Ana County			
Year	Judge	Year	Judge
1853-55	Richard Campbell	1863-68	John Lemon
1856	Pablo Melendres	1869	John Fietze
1856-59	Rafael Ruelas	1869-76	Pablo Melendres
1860	Anatasio Barelas	1877	Henry J. Cuniffe
1861	Thomas J. Bull	1878-79	Pablo Melendres
1861-62	Frank Higgins	1881	Maximo Castañeda
1862	John P. Deus	1899-1902	Albert J. Fountain
1863	Neponi Y. Ancheta	1903-06	Marcial Valdez

Table 7.4 Early Probate Clerks of Doña Ana County			
Year	Clerk	Year	Clerk
1853	Joseph H. Tucker	1876	Daniel Frietze
1854-59	James A. Lucas	1877-79	William T. Jones
1860	G. H. Oury	1879-84	Horace H. Stephenson
1861-62	Charles A. Hoppin	1885-86	Jesus S. Garcia
1863-65	James M. Taylor	1887-96	Horace H. Stephenson
1866-69	F. Bennett	1900	José R. Lucero
1870	Ygnacio Orrantia	1901-06	Isodoro Armijo

that the records were incomplete and sometimes completely missing. Since he published his work in 1907, his lists stop at the year 1906 and are presented in the last three Tables.

County Seats

When the New Mexico Territorial government created the County of Doña Ana on January 9, 1852 it named the town of Doña Ana to be its county seat, but on the last day of that year on December 31, 1852 transferred[13] the county seat to Las Cruces. La Mesilla, on the west side of the Rio Grande, was still in the process of being created at that time and being administered by the Mexican State of Chihuahua due to Bartlett's acceptance of latitude 32° 22' North as the southern boundary of the USA west of the Rio Grande. La Mesilla became part of the US when the Gadsden Purchase agreement was officially accepted in the Mesilla Plaza on November 16, 1854. The following year, on December 31, 1855, the New Mexico Territorial Legislature

13   C.W. Ritter. Mesilla Comes Alive, 2014. p142.

Table 7.5 Early Commissioners of Doña Ana County			
Year	Chairman	Commissioner	Commissioner
1876	Thomas J. Bull	Jacinto Armijo	Pablo Melendres
1877-78	Charles Lasinsky	John D. Barncastle	Pablo Melendres
1879-80	Guadalupe Ascarate	Eugenio Mareno	Sixto Garcia
1881-82	Carlos H. Armijo	Nicholas Galles	Amado Arvizii
1883-84	R. E. Smith	Benjamin E. Davies	Eugenio Mareno
1885-86	Mariano Barela	John D. Barncastle	Jacinto Armijo
1887-88	Thomas J. Bull	Leon Alvarez	Brigado Garcia
1889-90	George Lynch	George W. Mossman	Thomas J. Bull
1891-94	Tomas Gonzales	Numa Raymond	Leon Alvares Lopez
1895-96	Acheson McClintock	Charles Miller	Rosalio Baldonado
1897-98	Charles Miller	Rosalio Baldonado	Jesus Silva
1899-1900	Frank S. Oliver	Doyle Murray	Jesus Silva
1899	Frank S. Oliver	D. M. Sutherland*	Jesus Silva
1900	Frank S. Oliver	E. E. Day**	Jesus Silva
1901-02	W. B. Murphy	Charles E. Miller	Agapito Torres
1903-04	Charles E. Miller	Agapito Torres	Samuel Geck
1905-06	Richard Nietzschmann	Franscisco Jaramillo	Samuel Geck
*	Sutherland replaces Murray		
**	Day replaces Sutherland		

named La Mesilla[14] as the new County Seat of Doña Ana County, replacing Las Cruces.

La Mesilla held the County Seat for the next 27 years. [With the exception of the two years when it was the Capital City of the Confederate Territory of Arizona.] In 1865 The Rio Grande flooded and changed course from the east side to the west side of La Mesilla. However when the railroad came through the Mesilla Valley in the early 1880s, the owners of the land where the railroad wanted to place the depot in La Mesilla would not sell the land. When Don Jacinto Armijo offered his land in Las Cruces for the depot, the railroad was re-routed to that town. La Mesilla began a rapid decline in prosperity and in 1883 the County Seat was once again transferred to Las Cruces, where it remains to the present time.

---

14   D. G. Thomas. La Posta, 2013. p12.

Measures and Equivalents

The primary measure of length of concern to this work is the Spanish "vara". This measure originated in the Spanish era but continued to be used for surveying land throughout the Mexican period and into the early times of US jurisdiction. In this book, we have listed modern equivalents for most measurements in context, but this appendix will provide an opportunity to list out additional measures of length, area and volume which may be helpful when consulting some of the referenced material.

The information in this appendix has been gathered over a number of years by the author and is offered here without references, but much of the data is readily available through the internet.

Units of Length

Vara: The *vara* is a measure of length used in land surveys, but has varied in length in different regions and at different times.

generally accepted: 1 vara = 0.835905 meters

= 32.90964 inches

= 2.74247 feet

= 0.914157 yards

in Spain: 1 vara = 0.835905 meters since 1801.

in Texas: 1 vara = 33 1/3 inches = 0.92592 yards

= 0.846670 meters

in California: 1 vara = 33 inches = 0.916666 yards

= 0.8382 meters

League: The league is used for measuring longer distances and was typically the distance an army could march without resting. Historically there were several types of "leagues" including "legua legal", "legua comun" and "legua geographica" with varying lengths for each.

generally accepted: 1 league = 5,000 varas

= 4,178.52 meters

= 2.5963 miles

in Spain: 1 league = 6,666 2/3 varas since 1801

Palmo: A *palmo* is the distance between the thumb and the little finger when the hand is spread to its maximum extent.

1 palmo = 20.873 centimeters   (in Spain after 1801)

= 8.218 inches

Units of Area:

Labor: A *labor* is a measure of land surface and generally implies land lying along a river.

1 labor = 1000 varas x 1000 varas = 1 million varas^2

= 177.1 acres

League (area): A league of land measures 1 league (distance) x 1 league (distance) and typically implies land lying farther from a river.

1 league = 5000 varas x 5000 varas = 1 square league

= 25 million varas^2

= 4,427.5 acres

Fanega (area): A *fanega* is a measure of volume for measuring grain but was also used to specify the amount of land which could be sown with a fanega of grain.

1 fanega = 96 vara x 96 vara in Spain after 1801

= 80.2 meter x 80.2 meters

= 1.59 acres

Caballeria: A *caballeria* is a measure of land area probably originally intended for Spanish knights.

1 Caballeria = approximately 745 varas x 745 varas

= 552,960 varas^2

= 0.553 labors = 98 acres

Hacienda: A *hacienda* referred to a larger holding of land (as well as to the estate, itself) and usually was held by someone of high political importance.

$$1 \text{ hacienda} = 5{,}000 \text{ varas} \times 25{,}000 \text{ varas}$$
$$= 125 \text{ million varas}^2$$
$$= 22{,}142 \text{ acres}$$
$$= 34.6 \text{ sections} = 34.6 \text{ miles}^2$$

Units of Volume:

Fanega (volume): A *fanega* is a measure for determining the volume of dry material, such as grain. It appears that this term may have been used for "*media fanega*" or "half a fanega" at some times and some places.

$$1 \text{ fanega} = 1.58 \text{ US bushels}$$
$$= 1.966 \text{ feet}^3 = 3397.5511 \text{ inch}^3$$
$$= 55.7 \text{ liters}$$

Origin of Some Names

The origin of some of the place names that appear throughout this book have been controversial for quite some time. I will attempt to tell the major versions of the stories for a selected list of some of those places and give some rationale for choosing my favorite version. This may provide insight into the origin of the names but I hold little hope that it will eliminate the controversy associated with most of the names.

Doña Ana.

Curry and Nichols[1] in their 1974 book "Our Heritage, Our People" relate a legend about a lady who had lived and died in the region of Doña Ana.

> *She was so beloved by all, a headstone was made to mark her grave and it was inscribed, simply, "Doña Ana." No one seems to know where this stone was located, but the name of Doña Ana remains. Many people believe this is the way the town was named.*

There are two chief candidates for the identity of Doña Ana. One is Ana Robledo, the granddaughter of Pedro Robledo. Pedro and his two sons were traveling north with Juan de Oñate in 1598 when Pedro died and was buried at what came to be called *paraje Robledo* adjacent to the present ruins of Fort Selden. Ana Robledo apparently came south with Governor Otermín after the 1680 Pueblo Revolt and may have settled somewhere around the *paraje* Doña Ana. The second candidate for the village's namesake is Doña Ana Maria Nina de Córdova who is known to have had a sheep ranch[2] somewhere close by the same *paraje* probably circa 1800 if not before.

A different story is told by Maude Elizabeth McFie (Bloom) in her "A History of the Mesilla Valley-1903." One of the people she interviewed for her book was Pablo Melendres, Jr. and she thought his story of the naming of the village was the most credible. Melendres was the son of the first alcalde of Doña Ana and he, himself, had come to Doña Ana in 1843 when just a small boy. Melendres[3] told of some unknown or unspecified

1   Curry and Nichols. Our Heritage Our People, 1974. p 1.
2   http://www.explorenewmexico.biz, 1/31/2011. Acc 5/12/2014.
3   M. McFie. A History of the Mesilla Valley-1903. 1999. p 16.

woman named Ana of El Paso del Norte and how she had extracted a promise from some of the settlers of DA to name the colony after her.

> Pablo Melendres' story would imply that Doña Ana was named when the colonists arrived but apparently the *paraje* was named long before, perhaps even before Governor Otermín stayed[1] there on February 4, 1682 and where "we marched on the 4th to another place which they called[2] Doña Ana..." Melendres' version of the origin of the name is probably incorrect.

1   J. J. Bowden. Spanish and Mexican Land Grants, 1971. p 75.
2   Doña Ana County NMGenWeb PROJECT. Acc 5/12/2014

Las Cruces.

Maude McFie has recorded a story about the naming of Las Cruces told to her by Samuel G. Bean[4] shortly before his death in 1903.

> *In 1840, a party of forty Mexicans were on a journey from New Mexico to the State of Chihuahua with a train of pack mules on a trading expedition, as it was the custom every year to make these trips for the purpose of exchanging commodities.*
>
> *At the point where the town of Las Cruces now stands there was a fearful mesquite jungle where the Indians, who held high carnival in the wilderness of this valley, waited the coming of the unsuspecting party. They made the onslaught from ambush, and it was a "Custer Massacre," as not one of the forty Mexicans were left to tell the bloody tale.*
>
> *At that time there were no telegraph lines to wire the appalling news to kindred and friends, but they received notice by some means, and kind friends came and paid their last respects to the dead. Every spot of ground was marked where each bloody corpse was found by two boards nailed as the symbols of the holy cross. These crosses were standing here when I first came to the Territory in 1846.*

Another story is given by Rosemary Buchanan in her book entitled "The First 100 Years" published in 1961. After pointing out several other possibilities for the naming of the town,

4   M. McFie. A History of the Mesilla Valley-1903. 1999. p 40.

Buchanan[5] says:

> *No one quite knows the history of how Las Cruces got its name. Some say that on this spot in 1787 a party composed of a bishop, a priest, a Mexican Army colonel, a captain, four troopers, and four choir boys were murdered by Apaches, on their way north from Paso del Norte. ... In due course kindly hands performed the final and supreme act of charity by giving decent burial to the slain, and over each grave was placed a cross...*

Curry and Nichols[6] say only that Las Cruces was named "presumably in honor of the crosses placed on the graves of three missionaries who were massacred by the Indians."

On the other hand, C. W. (Buddy) Ritter[7] points out that "Las Cruces" may not have been named for "crosses" but, may have been named for "crossroads." Ritter maintains that an old east-to-west Indian trade route presumably to Picacho and points west ran basically along the present path of Highway 70 to Organ Pass crossing the north-to-south El Camino route probably somewhere along the present "Three Crosses Road" near its junction with Alameda Blvd. He also maintains that there is "virtually no direct evidence" for any of the above Indian attacks or on any specific group of crosses for which the town would have been named.

Whether the town was named for the crosses marking gravesites as in Samuel Bean's story or was named for being located near a crossroads per Ritter's assertion, the "las cruces" mentioned by Antonio Rey as marking the southern edge of the village Doña Ana (see Chapter 6) would seem to be the same spot. The location of the graves for the other Indian attacks (if they ever existed) are not sufficiently documented to say they were close enough to the present city of Las Cruces to be its namesake. I think that Bean's account is the most credible based on his being a near first-hand witness.

Tortugas.

The village of Tortugas (sometimes called the Pueblo of Tortugas) was the third village formed from the Doña Ana Bend Colony

---

5   R. Buchanan. The First 100 Years, 1961. p 9.
6   Curry and Nichols. Our Heritage Our People, 1974. p 81.
7   C.W. Ritter. Mesilla Comes Alive, 2014. p 67.

Grant and was presumably intended for the Indian population who no longer wanted to live around El Paso del Norte. Tortugas and Las Cruces were created about the same time and a great many Indians settled in Las Cruces, mostly south of the blocks laid out by Captain Sackett.

There is also some controversy of the origin of the name of Tortugas. Apparently the name of the village was originally "San Juan" but seems to have been popularly called "Tortugas" (meaning "turtles") since its early days. The most common explanation for its name is that it was named for "Tortugas Mountain" which is close by the village. The mountain was so named because its shape resembles a turtle when viewed from the north along the El Camino Real. However, Curry and Nichols report a story by Senora Maria Gonzales Carriere[8] who was born in Las Cruces in 1891. Her story states:

> *At the time the land was granted to the Indians... the vegetation farther south, near Tortugas, was more like that of a swamp. Brush-like willows grew everywhere and trees had thick, knobby roots that rose above the surface of the ground ... large turtles would come out to sun themselves on these roots and along the sandy banks. The people of Las Cruces would drive out now and then to amuse themselves by watching the turtles. This is the way the name of the settlement was changed.*

The name "Las Tortugas" appears on the 1855 Pope map of the Mesilla Valley (see Chapter 5) at the proper location of Tortugas. This cannot be taken as evidence that Senora Carriere's story about the turtles is wrong, but her conclusion concerning the name change is obviously incorrect.

---

8   Curry and Nichols. Our Heritage Our People, 1974. p 85.

References Cited

Adams, Eleanor B. *Bishop Tamaron's Visitation of New Mexico, 1760*. Albuquerque, New Mexico: University of New Mexico, 1954.

Anderson, George B. *History of New Mexico, Vol. 2*. Los Angeles, California; Pacific States Publishing Company, 1907.

Aranda, Dan. Personal Communication. Nov. 2, 2018.

Baker, Marcus. "Northwest Boundary of Texas" in *United States Geological Survey*. Washington, District of Columbia: Government Printing Office, 1902.

Baldwin, P.M. "A Short History of the Mesilla Valley" in *New Mexico Historical Review, Vol. 13, No 3, July 1938*. Albuquerque, New Mexico: University of New Mexico, 1938. https://archive.org/details/newmexicohistori01univrich.

Bancroft, Hubert Howe. "History of Arizona and New Mexico 1530 – 1888" in *The Works of Hubert Howe Bancroft, Vol. 17*. San Francisco, California: The History Company, 1889. http://www.vendio.com/stores/euriskodata/item/computers-tablets-networking-o/23-old-books-new-mexico-histor/lid=36971109.

Beck, Warren A. and Ynez D. Haase, *Historical Atlas of New Mexico*. Norman, Oklahoma: University of Oklahoma Press, 1969.

Bloom, Maude Elizabeth McFie. *A History of the Mesilla Valley - 1903*. Las Cruces, New Mexico: Yucca Tree Press, 1999.

Bowden, J.J. *Spanish and Mexican Land Grants in the Chihuahuan Acquisition.* El Paso, Texas: Texas Western Press, 1971.

Buchanan, Rosemary. *The First 100 Years.* Las Cruces, New Mexico: Bronson Printing Co., 1961.

Curry, Ella Banegas and Shan Nichols. *Our Heritage, Our People.* Las Cruces, New Mexico: Self Published, 1974.

DeLong, Sydney R. *The History of Arizona.* San Francisco, California: The Whitaker & Ray Company, 1905.

Dobyns, Henry H. Spanish Colonial Tuscon. Tucson, Arizona: University of Arizona Press, 1976.

Doña Ana Bend Colony Grant (web site). http://genealogytrails.com/newmex/ donaanabendcolony.html*****

Doña Ana Historical 2017 Calendar. Doña Ana Historical Preservation Committee, 2017.

Doña Ana Historical 2019 Calendar. Doña Ana Historical Preservation Committee, 2019.

Drexler, James J. *The Coronado Expedition to the Seven Cities of Gold.* Montrose, Colorado: Papaya Press, 2015.

Drexler, James J. *The Route and Ordeal of Cabeza de Vaca.* Las Cruces, New Mexico: CreateSpace, 2016.

Drumm, Stella M. *Down the Santa Fe Trail and into Mexico,* Lincoln, Nebraska: University of Nebraska Press, 1982.

Ferguson, Philip G. "Diary of Philip Gooch Ferguson" in *Marching with the Arm of the West 1846 – 1948* by Abraham Robinson Johnston; Marcellus Ball Edwards: Philip Gooch Ferguson. Glendale, California: Arthur H. Clark Company, 1936.

Frazer, Robert W. *Mansfield on the Condition of the Western Forts 1853-54*. Norman, Oklahoma: University of Oklahoma Press, 1963.

Frazer, Robert W. *New Mexico in 1850: a Military View*. Norman, Oklahoma: University of Oklahoma Press,1968.

Full Text: *El Camino Real de Tierra Adentro*. https://archive.org/stream/elcaminorealdeti2937palm/ elcaminorealdeti2937palm_djvu.txt.

Garcia, Mary Jane M. *An Ethnohistory of Doña Ana*. Las Cruces, New Mexico: New Mexico State University, 1986.

Hackler, George. *The March of the Mormon Battalion Through New Mexico*. Las Cruces, New Mexico: CreateSpace, 2016.

Jackson, Hal. *Following the Royal Road*. Albuquerque, New Mexico: University of New Mexico Press, 2006.

Keleher, William A. *Turmoil in New Mexico*. Albuquerque, New Mexico: University of New Mexico Press, 1952.

Kilcrease, Della J. *A Century of Memories*. Las Cruces, New Mexico: New Mexico State University, 1988.

Kiser, William S. *Turmoil on the Rio Grande*. College Station, Texas: Texas A&M University Press, 2011.

Kiser, William S.. *Dragoons in Apacheland*. Norman, Oklahoma: University of Oklahoma Press, 2012.

Long, John H, Ed. "New Mexico: Individual County Chronologies". in *New Mexico Atlas of Historical County Boundaries*. Chicago, Illinois: Newberry Library. 2007. https://publications.newberry.org/ahcbp//documents/ NM_Individual_County_Chronologies.htm.

MacNeish, Richard S. and Jane G. Libby. *Pendejo Cave.*
Albuquerque, New Mexico: University of New Mexico
Press, 2003.

McFie, Maude Elizabeth. *A History of the Mesilla Valley -
1903.* Las Cruces, New Mexico: Yucca Tree Press,
1999. *See also Bloom.*

Moorhead, Max L. *New Mexico's Royal Road.* Norman,
Oklahoma: University of Oklahoma Press, 1958.

Morehead, Max L. *Commerce on the Prairies by J. Gregg.*
Norman, Oklahoma: University of Oklahoma Press,
1954.

Owen, Gordon. *Las Cruces New Mexico Multicultural
Crossroads.* Las Cruces, New Mexico: Doña Ana
County Historical Society, 2005.

Pino, Pedro Boutista. *The Exposition on the Province of New
Mexico, 1812.* Santa Fe, New Mexico: El Rancho de
las Golondrinas, 1995.

Prince, L. Bradford. *Historical Sketches of New Mexico.*
Kansas City, Missouri: Ramsey, Millett & Hudson,
1883.
https://www.google.com/books/edition/Historical_
Sketches_of_New_Mexico/rxcWAAAAYAAJ?hl=en&g
bpv=1&pg=PA1&printsec=frontcover.

Proudfit, James K. "Doña Ana Bend Colony Grant, Surveyor-
General's Office Report No. 85" April 4, 1874 in *NM
State Records Center and Archives, Santa Fe, New
Mexico.* Spanish Archives of New Mexico I, Series
V; Surveyor General/Court of Private Land Claims
Records, 5.2 Surveyor General Case Files SG 85 –
Doña Ana Bend Colony. SANM Microfilm Reel 21,
frames 843 to 1131. Accessed through New Mexico
State University Library.
http://dev.newmexicohistory.org/filedetails.
php?fileID=24678#_ednref22.

Reff, Daniel T. *Depopulation and Culture Change in Northwestern New Spain. 1518-1764.* Salt Lake City: University of Utah Press, 1991.

Ritter, C. W. *Mesilla Comes Alive.* Las Cruces, New Mexico: Ritter Publications, 2014.

Roeder, Wilfried E. "New Mexico's Historic East Boundary" in *Antepasados.* Albuquerque, New Mexico: New Mexico Professional Surveyors, 1995.

Roeder, Wilfried E. "Perhaps the Most Incorrect of Any Land Line" in *Antepasados.* Albuquerque, New Mexico: New Mexico Professional Surveyors, 1995.

Roeder, Wilfried E. "The Boundary of All These Kingdoms" in *Antepasados.* Albuquerque, New Mexico: New Mexico Professional Surveyors, 1995. http://www.amerisurv.com/content/category/17/315/136/50/0/.

Smith, Ralph A. *Borderlander.* Norman, Oklahoma: University of Oklahoma Press, 1999.

Staski, Edward. "An Archaeological Survey of El Camino Real de Tierra Adentro, Las Curces – El Paso" in *International Journal of Historical Archaeology Vol. 8, No.4 (December 2004).* Springer, 2004.

Staski, Edward. "Some of What We Have Learned," in *Chronicles of the Trail.* Las Cruces, New Mexico: Quarterly Journal of the Camino Real de Tierra Adentro Trail Association (CARTA) , Vol 1, No 2, 2005.

Thomas, David G. *La Posta.* Las Cruces, New Mexico: Doc45 Publishing, 2013.

Torok, George D. "El Camino Real de Tierra Adentro through the Pass of the North, Part II" in *Chronicles of the Trail.* Las Cruces, New Mexico: Quarterly Journal of the Camino Real de Tierra Adentro Trail Association (CARTA), 2009, Vol. 5, No 2.

Torok, George D. *From the Pass to the Pueblos.* Santa Fe, New Mexico: Sunstone Press, 2012.

Wadsworth, Richard. *Forgotten Fortress.* Las Cruces, New Mexico: Yucca Tree Press, 2002.

Walker, Henry P. and Don Bufkin. *Historical Atlas of Arizona.* Norman, Oklahoma: University of Oklahoma Press,1979.

Wislizenus, A. *Memoir of a Tour to Northern Mexico. Senate Miscellaneous No. 26.* Wasington, District of Columbia: Tippin & Streeper, 1848. http://www.blackrange.org/The_Black_Range_Rag/ Blog__The_Natural_Observer/Entries/2016/8/23_ Entry_1_files/Memoir%20of%20a%20Tour%20 of%20Northern%20Mexico%20Connected%20 With%20Col.%20Doniphan%27s%20Expedition%20 in%201846%20and%201847%20-%20Friedrich%20- Adolph%20Wislizenus.pdf. Accessed 9/18/2018.

http://www.tshaonline.org/handbook/online/articles/hdelu. Acc. 6/23/2019

http://en.wikipedia.org/wiki/Tubac,_Arizona. Acc 6/26/2019.

http://parentseyes.arizona.edu/tubac/app2.htm. Acc 6/26/2019.

http://www.explorenewmexico.biz, 1/31/2011. Acc 5/12/2014.

http://www.nps.gov/tuma/learn/historyculture/timeline.htm. Acc 6/26/2019.

https://en.wikipedia.org/wiki/New Mexico meridian. Acc 7/29/2019.

https://en.wikipedia.org/wiki/Tucson,_Arizona. Acc 6/27/2019.

https://en.wikipedia.org/wiki/United_States_Court_of_Private_ Land_Claims. Acc 7/30/2019.

https://nmagp.genealogyvillage.com/donaana/sheriffs_donaana. htm, acc 8/28/19.

https://www.nps.gov/tuma/learn/historyculture/timeline.htm. Acc 6/26/2019.

Index

150   *Doña Ana*